# To Build a Better Teacher

# To Build a Better Teacher

*The Emergence of a Competitive Education Industry*

ROBERT GRAY HOLLAND

FOREWORD BY
MICHAEL POLIAKOFF

PRAEGER

Westport, Connecticut
London

**Library of Congress Cataloging-in-Publication Data**

Holland, Robert Gray.
    To build a better teacher : the emergence of a competitive education industry / Robert
Gray Holland ; foreword by Michael Poliakoff.
      p. cm.
    Includes bibliographical references and index.
    ISBN 0–89789–885–0 (alk. paper)—ISBN 0–89789–886–9 (pbk.)
      1. Teachers—Training of—United States.   2. Teachers—Selection and appointment—
United States.   3. Educational accountability—United States.   I. Title.
    LB1715.H63 2003
    370.71'1—dc21        2003045969

British Library Cataloguing in Publication Data is available.

Library of Congress Catalog Card Number: 2003045969
ISBN: 0–89789–886–9 (pbk.)

First published in 2003

Praeger Publishers, 88 Post Road West, Westport, CT 06881
An imprint of Greenwood Publishing Group, Inc.
www.praeger.com

Printed in the United States of America

The paper used in this book complies with the
Permanent Paper Standard issued by the National
Information Standards Organization (Z39.48–1984).

10 9 8 7 6 5 4 3 2

*For Allyne, Kristina, Amanda, Bobby, and Zoey*

# Contents

# *Foreword*

America enjoys at this moment an unprecedented opportunity to make great and lasting advances in teacher quality. There is no argument about the importance of this task. Research confirms what common sense tells us: of the factors over which we have control in education, teacher quality is by far the most important. Books, buildings, curriculum, and computers matter, but not nearly as much as the mind and heart of the school teacher. And there is real impatience that 20 years after *A Nation at Risk* identified grave teacher quality weaknesses, there has been neither improvement in outcomes nor the structural changes in teacher preparation that would lead to improvement.

How we achieve higher teacher quality is a hotly contested question. In his 1944 commentary, *Teacher in America*, the great humanist Jacques Barzun could only compare the situation that parents and students find themselves in when they try to evaluate the claims and counterclaims of various education professionals to the jurymen in *Alice in Wonderland*. And the analysis of the late Jeanne Chall in the *Academic Achievement Challenge* shows the real damage that the preposterous educational fads have wreaked on America's schoolchildren.

Thus it is timely for Robert Holland's new book to provide both crucial warnings against the failed nostrums of the past and encouragement to follow strategies that have both common sense and reliable data to recommend them.

The current, over-regulated systems of teacher certification, the monopoly education schools enjoy as providers of teacher training, and the rigid salary and personnel policies of schools have given us neither the supply nor quality we need in the nation's teaching force. Only when teaching is a profession where the top practitioners command the status and salaries they deserve and when school personnel policies no longer protect ineffective teachers will we achieve the teacher quality the nation's schoolchildren deserve. Shortages of qualified teachers will be significantly eased when a much wider pool of teachers is available, and this will happen when qualified candidates enter the classroom from so many different paths that "alternative" certification will no longer be an appropriate term. Programs to prepare teachers, whether education schools or "alternate" routes, should ultimately justify their existence—and funding—on the basis of the performance of the teachers they prepare.

President Bush signed the No Child Left Behind Act on January 9, 2002, with the hope and expectation that it will create a new culture of responsibility and achievement in our public schools. There are encouraging signs already that states are working cooperatively under the new federal guidelines. But this landmark law—as well conceived and crafted as it is—cannot succeed without the wisdom and dedication of the policymakers and school leaders whom the law entrusts with unprecedented flexibility and discretion. This brings us again to the important contribution that Robert Holland makes to education with this book.

Paradoxically, in No Child Left Behind, unlike the versions of the Elementary and Secondary Education Act that preceded it, the federal government minimizes its role in telling states and school districts how to spend the funds they receive. The nearly $3 billion for teacher quality initiatives in Title II do not come with requirements to spend a fixed amount on class size reduction or professional development. Instead, the new law describes a very broad range of teacher quality strategies, and then trusts the people closest to this nation's schools to make wise decisions.

That freedom comes with real accountability measures. No Child Left Behind will be true to its title: It expects results and has firm requirements for collecting reliable data on student progress and making that information accessible and transparent to every citizen in this nation. The law requires that within a few years all teachers be highly qualified. It requires steady progress toward student proficiency and the closing of the racial achievement gap in our schools.

It is crucial that we learn from past mistakes in education policy. I am pleased to see this thoughtful new report from an author who has a long record of championing education reform and individual rights.

I hope this book will be widely read and discussed, and that in the great tradition of this nation, it will help us to make the right local decisions, one by one, to strengthen teacher quality and better serve the children of this nation.

Michael Poliakoff,
former Pennsylvania Deputy Secretary of Education
and President of the National Council on Teacher Quality
Washington, D.C.
Summer 2003

# *Preface*

This is a book about building better teachers, not about tearing down the teachers we have. Education has been susceptible to waves of goofy ideas down through the years, but it has been my observation that teachers do not originate those fads. They tend to emanate from high-priced consultants, big companies with products to peddle, school bureaucracies, and school of education theorists with little or no connection to K–12 classroom reality. Frequently, level-headed teachers are the last line of defense against muddled thinking masquerading as innovation. I think of those California teachers who bootlegged phonics into their classrooms when that state so disastrously banished phonics from reading instruction in 1987 in exchange for Whole Language, a curious theory that assumes children will learn to read by osmosis if only they are surrounded by good books. (California subsequently has seen the error of its ways and confirmed the wisdom of those teachers who knew from firsthand experience what works.)

I come from a family of teachers. This book's dedication includes my daughter, Kristina, and my daughter-in-law, Amanda, who have taught in private and public elementary schools in Virginia. My wife, Allyne, taught creative writing and English in a public high school; as a young newspaper reporter, I met her amid the controversy when the local school board ignorantly sought to ban Harper Lee's *To Kill a Mockingbird* from her advanced reading list for seniors, even though she had cleared the assignment in advance with every single parent of every single student. That school board would rue the day it tangled with a teacher who had the courage of her convictions.

My gig had been journalism, mostly of the newspaper variety, before I became a Senior Fellow at the Lexington Institute in 1999.
Although I am not a professional educator, I have conducted writing
clinics for editors of high school papers and have taught university
journalism courses on an adjunct basis. That experience, together with
observing my family-member teachers at work, has given me a feel for
what it is like to face a roomful of young people expecting you to teach
them something (or at least to mark them "present"). I know enough
to realize that teachers have a demanding job full of daily challenges.

As it happens, virtually my entire journalistic career has been bound
up with education. My first assignment out of Washington and Lee
University was to cover the sad story of Prince Edward County's public
schools having been closed as a result of die-hard segregationists in
local power believing this somehow would stave off the U.S. Supreme
Court's order that public schools be desegregated with "all deliberate speed." The white children of that rural Virginia county went to
private school; the black children mostly did without—for four long
years. I went there as a cub reporter for the *Richmond Times-Dispatch*
the exciting fifth year when President John F. Kennedy and farsighted
Virginians like former Governor Colgate W. Darden, Jr., joined in
organizing a private school system, the Prince Edward Free Schools,
open to all comers but particularly geared to helping the deprived
African-American children catch up in their studies. (Today, there's a
happy ending in Prince Edward, with both the public and the private
schools peacefully integrated, doing well, and affording families a
measure of choice.) From that year of intensive education reporting,
I was hooked. I went on to become the education writer with the city
staff in Richmond, and when later I became an editorial writer and
opinion columnist for the *Times-Dispatch*, education stuck with me.
Although I could have written my weekly column about any timely
topic, I almost always devoted it to education.

When last I ventured into book writing, it was 1995 and parents
were in revolt in Virginia and across the nation over something called
Outcome-Based Education (OBE), a strange beast indeed. Again,
teachers did not concoct this monstrosity. It was the product of op-
portunistic consultants who found a way to repackage all that is bad
about progressive education and give it a corporate-sounding spin so
that big shots pushing restructuring through federal enactments like
Goals 2000 and School-to-Work could buy into it. The Outcomes
were about making kids attitudinally correct Collaborative Workers,
Global Citizens, Environmental Stewards, and the like, not about

teaching them to read and write and think for themselves. In talking to hundreds of outraged parents in the process of writing *Not With My Child, You Don't*, I found myself talking to almost as many teachers who were appalled at what the silly elitists wanted to foist on them. However, I found that almost without exception, teachers were not willing to be quoted by name. They felt in peril of losing their jobs. That is one of the saddest features of government-run education— that so many people who work in the system are intimidated into silence. It should not be that way in an enterprise devoted to encouraging informed, independent thought.

Writing *To Build a Better Teacher* in recent years, I found the situation different. Teachers were willing to open up and talk extensively and on the record about teaching philosophies, the quality of their preparation, and the possibilities for change in teacher training and certification. Maybe all that seemed less controversial than OBE, although the backdrop for today's discussion continues to be the education schools' power as a near-monopoly to push progressive ideology in the schools through their training of teachers.

I have many persons to thank for helping me produce this book. The list begins with the Chief Executive Officer at the Lexington Institute, Merrick Carey, who encouraged me to write an article on the topic of teacher certification for the journal *Policy Review*. Next, *Policy Review* editor Tod Lindberg did me a favor by pointing out I had done far too much preaching to the choir in my first draft. In a completely rewritten second draft, subsequently published, I tried to weigh competing points of view more judiciously, an approach I've tried to continue in this book. Finally, James R. Dunton, consulting editor at Praeger Publishers, read the *Policy Review* piece and suggested I consider writing a book on the topic. Jim has patiently answered my questions through the months as I've pondered the mysteries of preparing a manuscript for a major publisher. Back at the Lexington Institute, my colleague Executive Vice President Don Soifer has provided valuable technical help and general encouragement, and Annika Riegert, Julie Pearson, Kerry Finnegan, and Monica Kern cheerfully helped me download and print all manner of obscure research documents. I also am grateful for the Lexington Institute's permission for me to adapt papers I previously wrote for the Institute for inclusion in chapters 8 and 9 of this book. A big thanks goes also to Sylvia Crutchfield, Joyce Dimitriou, Amy Hornaday, and other friends at The Foundation Endowment who made it possible for me to try out some of my arguments at an education seminar at Windsor Castle in England, in the summer of 2001, and there to meet some of the brightest British minds on issues of education. The Foundation has supported my research since the early days of OBE.

A special word of gratitude goes to editors at three sprightly online services—Kathleen Carpenter at Teachers.net, Jimmy Kilpatrick at EducationNews.org, and John Stone at the Education Consumers Clearinghouse—who helped put me in touch with teachers and posted my frequent questionnaires soliciting observations and opinions. All three of these services are becoming indispensable media of education communication in the Internet age. Teachers.net allows teachers all over the United States and around the world to network regularly, to exchange ideas or just commiserate, and its *Gazette* runs timely and provocative articles. From deep in the heart of Texas, Jimmy Kilpatrick manages to post on EducationNews.org the major breaking news stories about education, as well as commentary, every day of the year. And John Stone's Clearinghouse brings educators and noneducators alike together to scrutinize education from a consumer's point of view, a perspective too often ignored by the public education monopoly.

Finally, I am grateful to all the teachers who talked to me at length, whether they agreed with my views or not. The thoughtful responses of many of them are quoted in this book. Dr. Cheri Pierson Yecke, Commissioner of Education for Minnesota and formerly Director of Teacher Quality and Public School Choice for the U.S. Department of Education, has helpfully provided perspective on these issues of reform. And of course, as always, the support of my favorite teacher, my wife, Allyne, has been indispensable.

# Introduction

To conclude that teachers of teachers tend to be like-minded believers that teachers should be facilitators of learning rather than transmitters of knowledge, it is necessary only to read their journal articles, attend their conferences, or review the descriptions of their courses in catalogs or on Web sites. One quickly comes to the conclusion that the professors of pedagogy are at odds with Mom and Pop, who want their children to acquire basic knowledge and skills in orderly, well-disciplined classrooms. You can sense that's true from reading a lot and talking to many people, but generalization always seemed risky.

It did, at least, until along came the single most important piece of research validating concerns about the overwhelmingly dominant mind-set of those who train most public-school teachers under near-monopoly arrangements with government bureaucracies. I am referring to the 1997 survey by the nonpartisan organization called Public Agenda, titled *Different Drummers: How Teachers of Teachers View Public Education.* That study provided revealing comparisons with earlier Public Agenda probes of the general public's expectations of the education system. The findings came from an organization that no one could dismiss as "far right" or even conservative. Public Agenda's founders in 1975 were Jimmy Carter's Secretary of State, Cyrus Vance, and a social scientist and polling expert, Daniel Yankelovich. In addition, some of Public Agenda's support comes from foundations that are considered to be left of center.

What Public Agenda found was a "staggering" disconnection between the professors of education's vision of teaching and what most parents, teachers, students, and civic leaders believe is desperately needed from the schools. Indeed, the survey exposed not a little professorial contempt for those who supply children and taxes to support the public schools, with almost eight in ten of the teachers of teachers (79 percent) certain that the public's ideas about learning are "outmoded and mistaken." While average adult Americans seek discipline and teaching of basics, such as correct spelling and grammar, only small percentages of education professors agreed. Just 19 percent deemed stressing correct grammar, spelling, and punctuation to be "absolutely essential," while even fewer (12 percent) put students being on time and polite in the "essential" column. As far as maintaining discipline and order is concerned, only 37 percent of the education professors thought that was essential (perhaps a sure tip-off that precious few of them have tried to control a K–12 classroom within the recent past).

Parents are interested in *content*: Has my child learned the multiplication tables and the story of the American Revolution? Public Agenda's study showed beyond doubt that most education professors are far more interested in *process*: Do students have the tools to construct their own knowledge? Almost nine in ten education professors (86 percent) said that when teachers assign mathematics or history questions, it is more important that the children grapple with the process of discovering the correct answer than that they actually come up with the right answer. Only 10 percent of the general public thought the use of calculators from the start would improve pupils' problem-solving prowess, but 57 percent of the education professors favored all-out calculator use. (Interestingly, only 23 percent of teachers agreed.)

While parents and taxpayers overwhelmingly want the data that objective tests generate, 78 percent of the education professors want schools to switch from tests to looking at portfolios of student work, a form of "authentic assessment" that relies heavily on subjective judgment by teachers. Parents and politicians like scores "because they're simple," a Los Angeles professor said contemptuously. By contrast, authentic assessment "provides a way to see different ways of knowing, more ways of solving problems."

In short, Public Agenda's data demonstrated that progressive, learner-centered ideals remain dominant in the schools of education, as they have for more than 80 years. In the words of one astute commentator, himself a professor of education, the teacher trainers "want classrooms in which the top priorities are positive attitudes toward learning and the presence of activities intended to encourage 'learning how to learn.' In their view, learning how to read, write, and do math is secondary to whether students find their classroom experience a satisfying one. Their ideal is schooling without schoolwork" (Stone, 1998a).

Now, the point of all this is not that there should be an ideological purge of schools of education to remove all traces of progressive thought; nor is the point even that the professors' ideas about helping children become problem solvers and lifelong learners are wholly wrong. (For goodness sake, isn't it possible to do *both*? Be sure that children have a sound foundation of basic skills and knowledge, *and* encourage them to be creative thinkers?) The point is that this like-minded monolith works in concert with the state education agencies to exert near-monopoly control over how teachers are prepared and what hoops they must jump through to be licensed to teach. Now, the education establishment's idea of "reform" is to make this control even more formidable by allowing no one to teach who has not passed through a school of education accredited, no longer by state bureaucrats, but rather by a national organization that avidly favors the progressive or learner-centered status quo.

Written from a journalist's perspective, this book is about exploring alternatives that will allow public education to be energized by teachers who bring a wealth of experience and subject-matter knowledge, as well as divergent philosophies of education, to the classroom. Education would benefit if teachers were evaluated and rewarded on the basis of how much they actually teach their pupils, how much they help them improve from year to year, according to objective measurements. For parents, teachers, and students who believe grades and tests have no place in a humane vision of education, there ought to be choice among schools that would permit them to patronize or work in progressive schools. The Public Agenda data indicate they would have a small market share, but they should be able to have that niche and demonstrate what they can do with it.

No one will have the freedom to seek better teaching and stronger education, however, until the intellectual stranglehold exerted by the teacher-education cartel is broken. This book looks at ways that might happen.

# CHAPTER 1
## *Facilitators at the Gates*

By and large, teacher training in the United States over the past century has not been about building better teachers.

The object instead has been to build better facilitators, non-authority figures who let children learn according to how their natural impulses may direct them.

That is the perhaps uncharitable view of those who believe fiercely that the primary role of the teacher is to transmit knowledge. Of course, the retort by those who believe just as passionately that the role of the teacher is to motivate a child to become an independent learner and to discover truths on his own is that to build a better facilitator *is* to build a better teacher. To facilitate learning *is* to teach.

So the debate goes back and forth, as debates over education means and ends have at least since Aristotle's and Plato's differing approaches to knowledge. No doubt such debate will never cease. However, in practice, as we shall see, many teachers blend competing approaches into their own practices, geared to what works best with particular students at different ages or stages of development.

Nevertheless, it seems fair to generalize a conclusion that teacher training has not had as an overriding objective the raising of academic achievement. Instead, major schools of education embrace a particular version of social justice as the central aim of education.

Because of their tendency to revere social aims more highly than intellectual pursuits, the schools of education have drawn heavy fire from critics inside and outside the major universities over the past 100 years. One critic who audited education courses at major universities across the land in the 1990s concluded that the teacher trainers had founded a "republic of feelings" that shunned the basic mission of transmitting knowledge to the young (Kramer, 1991).

Of course, faced with the daily realities of managing a classroom, many teachers modify or abandon the progressive approaches that were presented as holy writ by their professors of education. A study done in Ohio found that most elementary and secondary teachers use a mix of teacher-as-facilitator and teacher-directed practices (Chandler, 1999). However, if teachers are receiving training in an approach later found impractical, the tightly controlled system of teacher preparation is wasting much time and money that could be more efficiently directed.

A British professor's critique of this "wayward elite" lamented that "our society has been partly undermined by the belief that childhood is more important than knowledge, and equality more significant than excellence" (O'Keeffe, 1990).

Because of their naturalistic biases, the schools of education have drawn heavy fire from critics inside and outside the major universities over the past 100 years.

Some 75 years ago, that most acerbic of curmudgeons, Baltimore newspaperman H. L. Mencken, said that most education-school pedagogues "have trained themselves to swallow any imaginable fad or folly, and always with enthusiasm. The schools reek with this puerile nonsense. Their programs of study sound like the fantastic inventions of comedians gone insane. The teaching of the elements is abandoned for a dreadful mass of useless fol-de-rols" (Mencken, 1928).

The idea of naturalistic learning, sparked by French philosopher Jean-Jacques Rousseau (1712–1778), powerfully shaped the kind of child-centered pedagogy that Mencken and other hard-nosed critics eventually would deride. Rousseau had a leading role in the French Enlightenment and in shaping the Romantic movement in philosophy (Koetzsch, 1997). In his magnum opus, *Emile*, which was as much a wordy exposition on developmental psychology as on education methodology, Rousseau propounded the idea that the child is naturally good and is corrupted by the artificial environment and conventions imposed on him (Palmer, 2001). So statements like the following appear redundantly in *Emile*: "I am never weary of repeating: let all the lessons of young people take the form of doing rather than talking; let them learn nothing from books which they can learn from experience" (Foxley translation, 1993: 256).

Other education theorists—first Pestalozzi and Froebel, and later the likes of Piaget and Vygotsky—used Rousseau's ideas as the clay to mold a humanistic/progressive tradition that continues to have enormous appeal within education circles in the West, especially among those who train the teachers. In modern schools, progressive education is manifest in such practices as applied or discovery learning, project learning, the Whole Language approach to learning how to read, cooperative learning, authentic assessment, and the open classroom. That such ideas appeal to university intellectuals is not surprising, and the usefulness of certain of these ideas—learning by doing, for instance—in particular circumstances is beyond much dispute. But plenty of reasons exist to dispute the wisdom of insisting on naturalistic approaches for all when so many children lack the means to self-discover a foundation of skills and knowledge.

At the beginning of the twentieth century, immigrant parents desperately wanted their children to learn English and other elements of a traditional curriculum, such as American history, algebra, and science; however, progressive pedagogues swayed schools to reduce the number of children in the core subjects. In the name of social efficiency, they held that most students should be shunted to industrial or vocational studies for the good of society.

By the 1930s, the elitists in the education schools—influenced heavily by philosopher John Dewey (1859–1952), who incorporated Rousseau's thinking into a broader movement of secular humanism—were deeply committed to the idea that public schools should be agents of social transformation, as they were in the Soviet Union. Teacher trainers thereby became infatuated with the notion that teachers should be social engineers, not mere transmitters of time-tested knowledge (Ravitch, 2000).

As for the assumption that children possess a natural inclination to learn, and hence should be allowed to pursue their whims with a minimum of direction from the teacher, Dewey believed that children's natural curiosity would lead them specifically to become problem solvers. His disciples, then and now, have taken that to mean virtually all learning must be by doing; they disparage as "drill and kill" such activities as mastering the phonetic code, memorizing lines of poetry, or learning the multiplication tables by heart. William Heard Kilpatrick, teacher and writer-philosopher at Teachers College, Columbia University, was the person most responsible for popularizing student-centered learning. He directly trained an estimated 35,000 future education professors from 1918 to 1940 at Teachers College, and his tracts advocating project learning instead of a core curriculum spread his influence even more widely. Kilpatrick argued that knowledge is changing so rapidly that it is futile to teach required subjects; instead, children should simply learn how to look things up for themselves (Hirsch, 1996). To be sure, as Lawrence A. Cremin documented in his seminal study of progressivism in American education, Deweyites often misinterpreted and misapplied the ideas of the great theorist. Dewey was not a fan of project learning sans adult guidance. As early as 1926, he criticized as "really stupid" the deliberate lack of adult direction in the child-centered schools. According to Cremin, Dewey counseled that freedom is not something bred of "planlessness." Rather, "it is something to be achieved, to be systematically wrought out in cooperation with experienced teachers, knowledgeable in their own traditions. Baby, Dewey insisted, does not know best!" (Cremin, 1961: 234).

Nevertheless, the notion that a student's self-accessing information is more important than teachers' transmitting bedrock knowledge has gained new momentum in the Internet Age and permeates many of the programs recycled through education schools and school bureaucracies today. What's left unexplained is how a child can look up or cyber-surf for useful facts if he or she lacks the knowledge base to know where to look.

The student-centered approach travels under a variety of names, which tend to change as critics catch on to them: Outcome-Based Education in the early 1990s was one of the most deceptive, in that it implied outcomes academic in nature but delivered ones that were predominantly affective. In any event, "constructivism" now appears to be the pedagogical buzzword du jour. The Pacific Research Institute found that the California schools of education it studied proudly touted their embrace of constructivism (Izumi and Coburn, 2001). A look at school mission statements nationwide confirms that constructivism is the rage.

Tom Loveless of the Brown Center on Educational Policy at the Brookings Institution has described succinctly what constructivism is all about:

> The premise of constructivism implies that the knowledge students construct on their own, for example, is more valuable than the knowledge modeled for them; told to them; or shown, demonstrated, or explained to them by a teacher. Echoing the historical mantra of progressive education, constructivists argue that the essence of education—its means, ends, and motivating force—should be generated from within the learner, not decided by an external source. The teacher, the textbook,

the curriculum, indeed, the entire school and the external authorities it embodies are recast as facilitators in the student's construction of new knowledge, no longer the sources of it. (Loveless, 1998: 286)

Those in the opposing school of thought advocate teacher-centered instruction, which seems the essence of common sense to traditionalists or proponents of classical learning. This view, based on the wisdom of the ages, is that young pupils learn from teachers, who have a larger base of knowledge than do they. A mass of research exists that establishes beyond reasonable doubt that traditional, teacher-directed instruction is more effective in raising student achievement than is progressive, student-centered instruction. One of the most fair-minded and distinguished education researchers, Jeanne S. Chall, who was Emeritus Professor of Education at Harvard University Graduate School of Education until her death in 1999, meticulously analyzed a century's worth of data regarding the relative effectiveness of teacher-centered versus student-centered methods in raising student achievement. Her conclusion:

Traditional teacher-centered schools, according to research and practice, are more effective than progressive, student-centered schools for the academic achievement of most children. And that approach is especially beneficial for students who come to school less well prepared for academic learning—children of less educated families, inner-city children, and those with learning difficulties at all social levels. (Chall, 2000: 176)

Chall conceded that there are blends of the two approaches, and said that after teacher-centered instruction has given young children a good foundation of knowledge and skills, the more informal, progressive approach may well have increased usefulness when a child reaches high school. On the basis of her findings, she also recommended that schools of education put more effort into giving teachers and school administrators a good understanding of research and how they can benefit from it in their classrooms.

Yet critics charge that many education-school professors, who wield enormous clout over how teachers are trained and retrained after employment, persist in instructing prospective teachers in child-centered dogma as though there were no choice of philosophies or debate over them.

Something called Project Follow-Through, a federal program aimed at alleviating poverty through improved education, documents most starkly the refusal of the ed-school establishment to heed the results of legitimate research.

From 1967 to 1976, federal tax dollars paid for a longitudinal study of more than 20 differing approaches to teaching K–3 students from low-income homes. The experiment followed 70,000 Follow-Through students in 180 schools, and evaluated the effectiveness of approaches in which the children constructed their own meaning and knowledge versus those based on direct teaching of academic content and cognitive skills.

The clear result was that the most intensively teacher-centered model—a system called Direct Instruction, sponsored by the University of Oregon and developed by Siegfried Engelmann—was by far the most effective in raising the achievement of disadvantaged children to national norms, or close to them. Students in the student-centered or child-directed models (such as discovery learning, developmentally appropriate practice, open classrooms, and Whole Language) not only fell way behind their peers in teacher-directed classes but often performed worse in language, reading, spelling, and math than did the control group (Carnine, 2000).

Did this mass of evidence gathered by two reputable and independent organizations (Stanford Research Institute and Abt Associates) cause the education schools to reconsider their love affair with constructivism? For that matter, did subsequent studies, such as the 1999 report of the congressionally mandated National Reading Panel, which found teacher-directed instruction of phonemic awareness, the alphabet, and phonics to be essential for teaching most children to read?

Not in the slightest.

Numerous recent studies have confirmed the persistence of the child-centered bias of major schools of education. A comprehensive review by the Pacific Research Institute unearthed tons of evidence that the California State University (CSU) schools of education espouse the progressive approach as opposed to teacher-directed methods (Izumi and Coburn, 2001). In typical statements of mission, CSU-Dominguez Hills declared that "constructivist/cognitive approaches to teaching and learning inform our practice." CSU-Los Angeles asserted that its graduate education program "is based on a constructivist perspective of learning."

Quite revealing were the CSU ed-schools' required reading for prospective teachers. A multicultural text at Dominguez Hills states that "we cannot afford to become so bogged down in grammar and spelling that we forget the whole story," which the text summarizes as "racism, sexism, and the greed for money and human labor that disguises itself as 'globalization.'" (As will be noted in chapter 5, the leading multiculturalist and teacher-accreditation agencies are partners in a mission of politicizing teacher education.) Another required textbook at CSU-Fresno declares that "constructivist learning necessitates that students are perceived as active partners in framing the learning process. . . . No longer can teachers expect to be fountains of wisdom and convey knowledge to passive students." That would seem to leave little or no room for teacher-directed instruction. Yet another text for teachers in training, this one at San Francisco State, says that "there is no place for requiring students to practice tedious calculations that are more efficiently and accurately done by using calculators." (Such pronouncements raise the unanswered question of what soldiers in the field or even workers in an office are supposed to do when they've lost their calculators and have to do the math on their own.)

A Lexington Institute study of Web sites and catalogs found examples of the kinds of obstacles the major education schools place in front of would-be teachers (Holland, 2000). For instance, Teachers College, Columbia University, required of social studies candidates for a master's degree and for a recommendation for New York state teacher certification (grades 7–12) the completion of 38 education credits and an "integrative project." Among the required courses were the following:

- The Teaching of Social Studies
- Diversity and the Social Studies Curriculum
- The History of Social Studies Since 1880
- A course in special education
- A course in cognitive development
- Attendance at child abuse and drug/alcohol lectures
- Three courses in "professional development" outside the teaching field, such as developmental and cognitive psychology and bilingual/bicultural education
- A course in multicultural diversity, to which Teachers College "has a special commitment."

Conspicuously missing was any content—history, civics, geography— that might actually be taught to high school students in social studies classes.

In the same vein, the Kentucky Department of Education prescribed a set of performance criteria for aspiring teachers in the state-approved teacher preparation programs that appear to have little to do with whether a teacher knows English or history or can teach any English or history of value to his or her students. Here are some sample standards:

- Incorporates strategies that address physical, social, and cultural diversity and shows sensitivity to differences
- Establishes physical classroom environments to support the type of teaching and learning that is to occur
- Proposes learning experiences that are "developmentally appropriate" for learners
- Incorporates a multicultural/global perspective in content presentations
- Connects knowledge of the certified academic areas to real-life situations.

The University of Kansas College of Education helpfully stated its "assumptions" behind a curricular framework for teacher education, one being that "social justice and issues of equity are infused in major topics." New teachers must be able to "demonstrate basic skills in non-judgmental observation, critical inquiry, self-awareness, and reflective practices; have identified with teaching as a career path and a 'noble profession'; and demonstrate an awareness and interest in the issues and practices of education on a global basis." Again, there is much emphasis on subjective considerations, but scant emphasis on teaching core subjects and imparting knowledge.

A survey of education majors at Texas schools of education revealed a pervasive conviction that schooling should be centered more in the psyche than in the intellect (Horn, 1999). Compared to liberal arts majors, the prospective teachers were more likely to believe that social/emotional development is a more important goal for schools than academic development, and that instruction should be oriented more toward poor learners than high achievers or the gifted. Perhaps in addition to being influenced by their equity-focused professors, the education majors also felt empathy with the poorest K–12 students because they themselves brought woefully weak academic credentials to the universities. The study's author, University of Texas-Austin psychology professor Joseph M. Horn, found that across Texas, SAT scores for education majors and graduates were consistently the lowest of all collegiate majors—100 to 200 points lower in most cases.

That kind of aptitude deficit exists generally for education majors across the country. National Center for Education Statistics data reported in a 2002 U.S. Department of Education Report, *Meeting the Highly Qualified Teachers Challenge*, noted that among college graduates who majored in education, only 14 percent had SAT or ACT scores in the top quartile. That compares with 26 percent of social sciences majors and 37 percent of those who majored in mathematics, computer science, or the natural sciences. Interestingly, 25 percent of uncertified teachers ranked in the top quartile on their college entrance tests, as did 33 percent of private-school teachers.

In yet another of the most populous and influential American states, New York, a blistering journalistic critique of education-school giants like Teachers College, Columbia University, City University of New York, and Hunter College found them in the grip of an Anything But Knowledge dogma. Writing in *City Journal*, Heather Mac Donald observed, "Schools are about many things, teacher educators say (depending on the decade)—self-actualization, following one's joy, social adjustment, or multicultural sensitivity—but the one thing they are not about is knowledge" (Mac Donald, 1999).

As a journalist, Mac Donald made the sacrifice of sitting through hours of education classes. In one, the professor explained she would be "getting the students to develop the subtext of what they're doing," which turned out to be a "chain reaction of solipsistic moments." She asked the class to write for seven minutes on each of three questions: "What excites me about teaching?" "What concerns me about teaching?" And then the one steeped most in the affective, Anything But Knowledge style: "What was it like to do this writing?"

Then the professor asked the students to reflect. "What are you hearing?" A student spoke the obvious, "Everyone seems to be reflecting on what their anxieties are." The professor quickly translated that into ed-speak: "So writing gave you permission to think on paper about what's there." (Mac Donald observes what anyone exposed to years of reading education journals or attending education conferences can confirm: "Ed-speak dresses up the most mundane processes in dramatic terminology—one doesn't just write, one is 'given permission to think on the paper'; one doesn't converse, one 'negotiates meaning.'") Soon the class was divided into small groups—a staple of today's version of progressive education—and they had picked up the ed-speak. Asked how they "felt" in the small groups, they gave responses such as "It shifted the comfort zone"; "It was just acceptance; I felt the vibe going through the group"; "I felt really comfortable; I had trust there."

These feel-good sessions so typical of ed-school seemingly have nothing to do with teaching seventh graders about the writing of *The Federalist Papers* or the causes of the Great Depression, or indeed about much of anything at all. This is the ultimate triumph of process over substance.

There are, it should be noted, schools of education that are not devoted to progressive education and that instead exhibit dedication to the life of the mind. But they are the exceptions. One is Boston University's (BU) School of Education, where the undergraduate SAT combined average for entering freshmen is about 1260. The national average for schools of education is about 950. BU's education faculty has many top-flight scholars, including historian Paul Gagnon and Steve Tignor, a philosopher who takes a "great books" approach to teaching about the cultural foundations of education. Edwin Delattre, the Dean Emeritus of BU's education school, says that shortly before he became Dean in 1991, he asked the head of the primary overseer of teacher-training institutions—the National Council for Accreditation of Teacher Education (NCATE)—if it "would ever establish any substantive intellectual standards for accreditation rather than mere process requirements that express nothing but NCATE board member prejudices." Receiving no assurance, Dean Delattre withdrew his school from NCATE. He finds it regrettable that the Massachusetts Board of Education has voted to require NCATE accreditation for public schools of education, but "few of the academically powerful private universities here . . . including Boston University, will have anything to do with NCATE."

The progressive methodology—and schools of education perpetuating it—do have their earnest supporters. Alfie Kohn is a leading voice for progressivism, and Linda Darling-Hammond is the most insistent advocate of a guaranteed role for ed-schools as part of a tightly controlled system of teacher licensing.

Kohn lectures widely in the academic community and writes prolifically in the popular and trade press, attacking what he sees as retreats from the progressive tradition caused by political pressures to impose learning standards on the schools. Among his multiple targets are grades, tests, phonics, school choice, spelling bees, indeed competition in *any* form. He fears progressivists are backsliding on cooperative learning because of the pressure on schools to produce results.

In a 1999 interview with *Independent School*, Kohn disputed the idea that teacher as facilitator amounts to a laissez-faire approach to teaching, calling that "a caricature of progressivism kept alive by traditionalists who want to make their own stultifying methods look better." He continued:

> The best teachers are vitally active and involved, but not in propelling students toward the right answers. Not in filling them full of facts. Not in giving them worksheets that consist of naked numbers or disconnected sentences in which the point is to circle vowels or verbs. The teacher starts with the kids and then gently challenges them, subtly disorients them, throws them off balance with new ideas that the students have to struggle to reconcile with the way they'd been looking at things. This is really hard, of course. It takes effort and talent to work with kids to explore controversial issues, to design interdisciplinary projects with them, to assess their understanding by watching and listening instead of giving quizzes. (Thuermer, 1999)

Linda Darling-Hammond, a professor of education at Stanford University and (previously) Teachers College, as well as the founding Executive Director of the National Commission on Teaching and America's Future, is the prime advocate for bolstering the schools of education—with their student-centered pedagogy intact—as the gatekeepers to the teaching profession. Her vision of reform is to make the monopoly in teacher preparation and certification even more formidable.

No doubt she is sincere in her belief that it is essential to require future teachers to have a thorough grounding in schools of education that operate on a pattern ratified by national accrediting bodies. "The knowledge professionals need in order to make sound decisions," she wrote in collaboration with a national accrediting mogul, "is transmitted through professional education and by initiation through supervised clinical practice under the guidance of experts. This process requires that organizations of professionals achieve a consensus about what is worth knowing and how it can best be transmitted and that they then use these judgments as the basis for regulating professional preparation programs and entry standards" (Darling-Hammond, Wise, and Klein, 1999: 17).

That statement suggests a top-down vision of education as a static enterprise with a settled canon of best teaching practices as decreed by elitists who may not have been in a classroom in years. Furthermore, it suggests that one centralized authority properly may withhold a license to teach until a candidate is thoroughly grounded in the One Best Process. Of course, such monopoly control prevails only on the elementary and secondary levels. In American colleges and universities, including those where great teaching takes priority over research, professors are hired on the basis of their command of an intellectual discipline, not their having survived hundreds of hours of mandatory courses in arcane theories of education.

Under the prevailing K–12 system, Milton Friedman, Nobel Prize winner in economics, could not qualify to teach high school economics. Nor could Nobel laureate Steven Weinberg, a physicist, stand in front of a K–12 science class. Both scholars have been distinguished teachers at some of the most prestigious institutions of higher learning in the world. Vann Woodward, famed historian, couldn't be fully certified to teach history. Nor could famed diplomat Henry Kissinger receive a state certificate to teach children about twentieth-century world history.

Surely there are more rational ways to build better teachers for our nation's elementary and secondary schools.

# CHAPTER 2

# Teachers on Teaching

By no means do all teachers follow the wishes of ed-school professors that they be facilitators, or constructivists, who coax children into discovering or constructing their own meaning.

Many of them find through their own reading or their own trial and error in the classroom that their children need lessons presented to them in a logical, sequential, systematic way. The kids thrive on structure, which all too often is sadly lacking in their home life.

These are teachers who teach directly. They have a game plan, and they stick to it. Years later, they are often the teachers remembered as sticklers for detail and tough taskmasters. Not infrequently, we remember them as our best teachers, though they may not have been our favorite teachers at the time.

One paragon of teacher-directed instruction is Donna Garner, a teacher for 27 years in Texas public schools. She now teaches English and Spanish at a small Christian school.

Donna is not keen on the idea that children will absorb what they need to know if they are left largely to their own devices, as in a Whole-Language classroom, or that they will necessarily learn even if seemingly assigned a load of work to do.

On the writing of compositions, she says:

It is not enough for a student to be assigned many compositions to write. It is not enough for students to write in their journals daily. It is not the quantity but the quality of writing assignments that counts. Unless a student is explicitly and directly taught correct grammar/punctuation/spelling and unless he is then held accountable on his papers to implement correct writing, I do not believe that students' sentence structure will improve appreciably.

Students must correct their writing mistakes, and teachers must insist that they then rewrite their papers and incorporate those revisions. Otherwise, Donna Garner has observed, students will simply glance at their corrected, graded papers without trying to learn from their mistakes.

More generally, Garner is convinced that the content of students' papers will not improve "until they develop a foundation of knowledge upon which to construct their elaborations." No assertion offends progressive purists more than that one. "Teachers must," Garner says, "quit awarding students high grades when they have done nothing but simply emote their own opinions without having any substance in their compositions."

Donna Garner strongly believes that children must be taught basic skills and a foundation of knowledge before they can originate and analyze. Sequential, systematic instruction is particularly vital in English/Language Arts/Reading, because these disciplines constitute the foundation for all other learning.

Because of her outstanding record as a teacher, Garner won official appointment from the Texas Education Commissioner in the summer of 1995 to serve on a writing team for the English/Language Arts/Reading (ELAR) component of the Texas Essential Knowledge and Skills (TEKS), the Lone Star State's academic standards. But she and several other classroom teachers found that the state standards were heading not in the direction of explicit grade-by-grade standards but instead toward grade clusters emphasizing a constructivist approach with students learning largely by cooperating to do myriad projects. Garner and a number of other classroom teachers were so alarmed that they split off in 1997 to write their own set of proposed standards that came to be known as the Texas Alternative Document (TAD). Garner was the lead writer. Against all odds, TAD garnered so much support in Texas that it very nearly supplanted the official TEKS, which took $9.5 million to produce versus the $15,000 the teachers spent from their own pockets and a few supporters' donations to produce TAD. The teachers' revolt did result in some minor modifications of TEKS, which became the basis of the education reform touted by George W. Bush as Texas governor and now as U.S. president. However, the ELAR portion of TAD became even more of a model for many standards committees, schools, and teachers around the country, and is still widely used.

TAD's writers, experienced teachers all, were among the first educators in the country to draw on the seminal research on the teaching of reading conducted by Reid Lyon of the Child Health and Human Development branch of the National Institutes of Health. Lyon's research, which in the late 1990s won acclaim as the soundest peer-reviewed empirical research in the field, has documented that children need to be systematically taught phonemic awareness and decoding skills in order to learn to read well. The report of the National Reading Panel in 2000 drove home this point after panelists reviewed 100,000 studies of reading instruction done since 1966 and found the essential elements for teaching all children to read to be (1) phonemic awareness, (2) phonics, (3) fluency, (4) vocabulary, and (5) text comprehension (NRP, 2000). The No Child Left Behind Act of 2001, Bush's reform of federal education law that passed Congress with strong bipartisan support, requires more than 100 times throughout its 1,000-plus pages that subsidies go only to school programs that are supported by "scientifically based research." One result should be that TAD-like systematic phonemic awareness and phonics will become far more prevalent in federally funded reading programs than has been the case.

The TAD guidelines for teaching reading and English are richly detailed at each grade level. Starting in kindergarten, the focus goes first to listening, speaking, pre-reading, and pre-writing activities. For instance, teachers expect the children to listen to notable literary selections that are rich in vocabulary, such as the nursery rhymes "Mary Had a Little Lamb" and "The Little Red Hen," and *Winnie-the-Pooh* and *The Velveteen Rabbit*. Then the children are to discuss the meanings of words and concepts from the selections, describe mental pictures of settings and characters, retell selections, recite/sing rhymes and songs, and so on. These early activities build a foundation for others to develop syntactic awareness (the rudiments of grammar) and then the critical skill of phonemic awareness, an understanding that the spoken word consists of a sequence of elementary sounds. Even at age five, children can begin orally blending words into syllables, identifying words that begin with the same sound, reciting or even generating rhymes, segmenting words into phonemes, and finally copying the teacher in making the 44–45 sounds (phonemes) of American English. From this critical base of phonemic awareness, children can begin to take the next big steps toward knowing the alphabet by heart and grasping letter-sound associations and word attack skills. By the end of kindergarten, they are identifying the story lines and main ideas of literature rich in vocabulary that is read to them, and even reading aloud themselves simple texts in which no more than one to ten words are difficult for the child.

They are ready to read.

Of course, many in the progressive Thoughtworld are horrified at the thought of teachers directing children so meticulously in their first steps to reading. Donna Garner's approach certainly is a far cry from the philosophy of one of the pioneers of progressive education, A. S. Neill, who wrote in *Summerhill* (a book about his freewheeling English school of the same name) that "to impose anything by authority is wrong. The child should not do anything until he comes to the opinion—his own opinion—that it should be done" (Palmer, 2001: 1). The most ardent proponents of Whole Language, which began to dominate American reading instruction in the mid-1970s, are only somewhat less deferential to the child than was Neill. They contend children can pick up phonemic awareness, phonics, spelling, and other tools of language naturally—that is, without adult-directed practice. Explained one reading expert (by way of exposing its blatant fallacies), this is the ideological mind-set behind Whole Language: "Natural learning is playful, incidental, and easy. Phoneme awareness will happen if children play rhyming games; spelling will happen if children write; word recognition will happen if children follow the print as the adult reads; and comprehension will happen if children's curiosity is piqued. The teacher needn't follow a structure or a sequence; she is to share, guide, and facilitate as the child discovers how reading works" (Moats, 2000: 10).

What of education beyond initial reading instruction? Students in upper grades? To what extent does a good teacher facilitate, and to what extent does she or he directly teach? While some children may need structure, do not others respond well to invitations to direct their own learning? Donna Garner is on one side of the great divide in education: Should the teacher be a facilitator of learning or should the teacher be the director of learning? Of course, the choice is not absolute; many teachers do some of both. But on the other side of the divide (the left side, one supposes), there are thoughtful advocates of the teacher-as-facilitator model.

A survey of teachers undertaken nationwide in preparation of *To Build a Better Teacher* indicates that while teachers colleges tilt toward the teacher-as-facilitator/learner-centered model of instruction, some teachers depart from theory and teach directly when experience teaches them what their children need; however, there are those who find the learner-centered guidance helpful in their teaching. In fairness, many of those who favor the facilitator model do not do so to the point of tolerating anarchy in the classroom. Instead, they try to engage students in being serious, active learners. In fairness also, the teachers surveyed did not universally pan their education courses. They found some of the how-to instruction useful. The largest point of agreement among teachers of widely varying philosophies was that student teaching under the tutelage of an experienced teacher was a highly valuable component of teacher preparation and that it should be expanded.

Nettie Griffin, an elementary teacher in Illinois with seven years' experience, is among those who found the theory classes in education school far too one-sided in their affection for progressive ideology. "They drilled into my head the learner-centered approach, which is nice in theory, and I followed it for four years until I had my epiphany." Griffin said she taught Whole Language until realizing that "it doesn't really work." A teacher should be "the director of learning and not just a facilitator," she said, but direct teaching remains child-centered when the teacher is dedicated to doing what is best for the children. Children should be "independent thinkers," she continued, "but they should not be choosing their own curriculum."

By contrast, Emily Williams, a Smith College graduate who teaches kindergarten in the Bronx and who is in the process of earning a master's in elementary education at Manhattanville College, notes that her education professors "mostly used a teacher-as-director approach to teach us but favored using a teacher-as-facilitator approach in working with children." Currently in her first year of full-time teaching (after being an assistant for five years), she said her own philosophy is "developing and changing every day." Her stated philosophy reflects in part the teachings of L. S. Vygotsky and Jean Piaget, the Russian and Swiss theorists widely quoted in schools of education for their advocacy of student-centered learning. This is how Williams thoughtfully expresses her convictions about learning:

> Education should make us better people on many levels—social and emotional, as well as that of intelligence. Students need to learn more than how to read a book. Students need to learn how to write, create, and use information in the world around them. Education should be exciting, interesting, and challenging. It should broaden our abilities,

experiences, and knowledge. Education should be based on the needs of those being taught. Education should be in part a guided endeavor, and in part a personal endeavor. As educators, we want students who will become lifelong learners—reading, experimenting, and questioning long after school is over. Education should prepare us to be productive members of society. Education should make the tools for individual growth readily accessible whenever the student needs them. Vygotsky calls this the Zone of Proximal Development. [The ZPD theory holds that "psychological development depends upon outside social forces as much as upon inner resources" (Palmer 2001).]

Each student's zone is at a different level, and it is important that the teacher provides the tools and the activities that allow the student to learn within this zone, [because] it is there that the most growth can occur. Education should teach us about our emotional, social, cultural, and physical surroundings. Education should allow children to thrive through accomplishment—doing something for the first time, taking a risk, feeling involved, feeling physically and emotionally safe, and, most importantly, feeling school is a great place to be! Education should [quoting Piaget] "create men and women who are capable of doing new things, not simply repeating what other generations have done—men and women who are creative, inventive, and discoverers, [who] have minds which can be critical, can verify [rather than] accept what is offered."

It would be hard to be blasé in the face of such exuberant idealism. Surely a teacher so obviously dedicated to children could make a difference for the better in many lives. The ends of student-centeredness she espouses—developing people who can think for themselves—are unexceptionable. Still, one cannot help but wonder if such an idealistic teacher will have moderated her devotion to the theorists after three or four years of dealing with classroom realities. Of course, Williams herself acknowledged that her philosophy is being shaped every day in the classroom.

Ten-year teaching veteran Camille Farrington, who teaches humanities at the Young Women's Leadership Charter School in the inner city of Chicago, is another enthusiastic, insightful teacher who takes to heart what she has learned in schools of education about creating a student-centered learning environment. After earning a bachelor's degree in Women's Studies at the University of California-Santa Cruz, she has completed a year of graduate course work in education at Mills College in Oakland (where student teaching began the first week of school and continued yearlong, a focus she found most helpful), and at Berkeley and the University of Wisconsin-Madison.

"My own philosophy of education was shaped very significantly by my teacher education courses and professors," said Farrington. "I don't think children 'acquire' knowledge and skills unless they themselves are doing and creating something that means something to them and that actively involves them." Charter schools operate with a degree of autonomy within public-school systems and, at their best, provide parents, students, and teachers with choices among a variety of approaches to learning. Farrington's school is one of the few girls-only public schools in the country and has as a principal objective of overcoming whatever barriers exist to young women wishing to excel in mathematics, science, and technology.

Another thoughtful viewpoint comes from a 29-year veteran of teaching, David Frederick of Salinas, California, who has taught K–5, and has served as a mentor teacher and a trainer of student teachers. Frederick considers himself a constructivist, which he explained as follows:

> I believe that each of us has to construct our own ideas, that learning takes place in the mind, not on the workbook page, and that learning isn't like exercise because the mind isn't a muscle. I studied Piaget in college but it meant little to me until I started to see how it applied to real learning in my own classroom. It is most difficult to "acquire" knowledge in some rote fashion if it isn't connected to something meaningful. That doesn't exclude being taught some skills and knowledge, but it does mean that teaching needs to be more engaging than rote drill and the seat work common in most schools. By that I mean that children should do projects and play games while spending a small part of their day learning "facts" of one kind or another.

Frederick believes he received a good exposure to both the learner-centered and the teacher-centered perspectives while taking graduate courses in education at Fresno State, but he added that "professors tend to be somewhat more idealistic, and, therefore, more 'progressive.'" He expressed, however, a criticism common among teachers of both the traditional and the progressive perspectives: that a good deal of his education course work, though potentially valuable, was insufficiently specific. It "did not seem to relate to anything real," Frederick recalled. When he began teaching, "I could only vaguely remember that I'd learned this and that. Also, I didn't feel that enough emphasis was placed on learning disabilities and dealing with difficult children and specific emotional problems. Educational psychology was more about very general human psychology issues. No one could have prepared me for the amount of social welfare work that teaching involves.

"When I went through the academic hoops to become a teacher, a noneducation major was required in California. I think that was good. A few undergraduate education courses were taken along with the classes of my major and minor.

"I greatly favor an internship model. The graduate would work, perhaps with an experienced teacher, and be paid. Meanwhile, he/she could take classes over the Web. Classes should not contain any busy-work whatsoever. All 'work' would be directly related to the teaching job."

George T. Viglirolo completed his undergraduate work at the exemplary Boston University School of Education (mentioned in chapter 1) and spent much of his career teaching English at Brookline High School, where he was a Massachusetts Teacher of the Year finalist in 1993–1994 and recipient of the Harvard Prize Book Award for Excellence in Teaching. He retired from full-time teaching in July 2001, but continues to work part-time at Brookline. Viglirolo has some well-thought-out views on the Great Debate over teaching methods, which he doesn't think should be a debate at all. Learner-centered versus teacher-centered is a meaningless dichotomy, he contends, "because good teaching requires both approaches, as well as a combination of others."

The teaching/learning experiences, says Viglirolo, "proceed along complex, sinuous paths." What is needed is a coherent approach that integrates techniques and strategies in all academic disciplines. "One such model, for example, is Mortimer Adler's Paideia Proposal, which organizes curriculum into different types of teaching and learning: the acquisition of knowledge (such as language, literature, and the other humanities) through 'didactic' teaching; the development of skills (such as reading and writing, speaking and listening, etc.) through 'coaching'; and the appreciation and understanding of ideas through seminars and the 'Socratic method.' Just as a carefully planned sequence of skill development and knowledge acquisition is essential to mastery learning, so, too, is opportunity for making choices essential to full appreciation and understanding." And in that connection, he quotes an essay by the late professor, and commissioner/bard of baseball, A. Bartlett Giamatti, in the July 1980 issue of *Harper's,* titled "The American Teacher":

> No good teacher ever wants to control the contour of another's mind. That would not be teaching, it would be a form of terrorism. But no good teacher wants the contour of another's mind to be blurred. Somehow the line between encouraging a design and imposing a specific stamp must be found—and clarified.

John Tuepker is a former Peace Corps volunteer (Sierra Leone in West Africa, 1967–1969) who now teaches history and geography in Long Beach, Mississippi. (He also has been a local and state leader of the American Federation of Teachers, the second largest teacher union behind the National Education Association.) Tuepker has honed his own philosophy of teaching from his experience as a student and his observations during 14 years of teaching as to what is necessary in the classroom. "The teacher must be the leader of the class," Tuepker stressed. "There is a curriculum that must be covered and knowledge to be gained. I recognize the importance of a certain process [that might be called] 'teaching *how to learn* history' as well as the actual historical knowledge transmitted. I do not lecture, except to cover and organize material that students did *not* get from previous learner-centered classes. Students like organization. They like high standards and knowing that they earned their grade and that it was a real accomplishment. They recognize a teacher who has overwhelming knowledge of a subject, loves his work, and appreciates the students' efforts and accomplishments."

Nevertheless, Tuepker does not consider "facilitating" to be a dirty word.

> I do some facilitating—quite a lot, in fact. But it is in the traditional context, such as when we discuss the extensive homework. I ask questions leading to deeper thinking. I don't spell words for students, but make them look them up in the textbook. . . . They draw maps by themselves. They take extensive notes on videos by themselves. I grade the work, which ensures that all students, at least those who want to pass, will do it. That is all facilitating. But I do not like "cooperative learning"—the inefficient exchange of misinformation, and social hour—or "project method" (who has time for 30 students all doing a project, reporting on it to the class, discussion of it, correction of misleading or omitted information?), or social promotion, which is what the progressive method almost always leads to.

Don Crawford, who has taught for 11 years in K–12 schools in California, had a B.A. in psychology when he began graduate work in education at California State University at Los Angeles. Professors in special education (Crawford's specialty) were more teacher-centered than the regular education professors, he noted, but added, "This was back in the mid-1970s, so it wasn't as bad then as it is now." The education methods courses "should have been useful—but weren't," Crawford recalled. "I was teaching part-time in parochial school at the time I was taking classes, and I knew I needed to learn something—but it wasn't in the required course. [There was] a lot of make-work, but little immediately practical or useful—long on philosophy, short on specifics."

As for philosophy, Crawford said not until he reached the doctoral program at the University of Oregon, with its cluster of education professors who champion Direct Instruction, did he find teaching ideas compatible with his own. "I'm a Direct Instruction trainer, a fire-breathing true believer," he said. "Skills are essential. Fluency in basic skills and a fund of basic knowledge are both necessary prerequisites for being able to do 'critical thinking' and [to] express oneself clearly."

Core Knowledge schools that use a curriculum developed by cultural literacy advocate E. D. Hirsch, Jr., provide another productive venue for teachers who believe that transmitting knowledge in a systematic way is an important duty of teachers. Peggy Downs, a third-grade teacher at Peak-to-Peak Charter School in the Boulder Valley district of Colorado, believes that students must have a base of facts and general knowledge before engaging in fruitful critical thinking. She said her classroom experiences, as well as the works of such authors as Diane Ravitch and Hirsch, have influenced her teaching philosophy.

Downs said she earned a liberal arts degree in 1984, and then returned to school in 1990–1991 to gain her education certification. Taking a broad spectrum of undergraduate courses in a variety of disciplines was, she believes, "excellent preparation for teaching Core Knowledge." However, she found that her education professors at the University of Colorado-Boulder espoused the "Whole Language/child-centered philosophy exclusively. My approach is strongly teacher-directed and I was often at odds with my classmates and professors."

Some education courses "were helpful to a limited extent," Downs said. However, "some were a complete waste of time. Why is it that we spent an entire three-credit semester course on special education for severely handicapped students and exactly one afternoon on how to write objectives for learning? Why did our Reading Methods course spend whole afternoons discussing *Reading Rainbow* and not a single lesson on phonics or how kids learn to read? Why did our Math Methods course show us little games with base-10 cubes and counters, but never teach us what to do for a child who can't understand how to tell time?"

Patricia Reese, an Indiana teacher with 23 years' experience, found an experience during her years as a student at Purdue University's school of education to be highly instructive, though perhaps not in the way intended by course designers. When she entered the ed-school in 1977, she recalled:

> I was required to take a course called the Open Concept School. (The course had a textbook that went by the same name.) We were required to spend three hours a week observing and helping teachers in a school that was using this system. The walls had been torn down and it was one huge room [comparable to] the size of a gym. Students (elementary) decided what areas they wanted to attend. Some children would go to math first, others [to] reading, and some to art or music. Some students who didn't like math never ended up there. Teachers were frustrated. It was wild. There were many discipline problems. The idea behind this was that some students would do better and would like school if they were given the opportunity to decide their own day.
>
> When I was a senior, I was assigned to this same school for tutoring reading students. Guess what? The walls were back.

Even though most of her education professors were of the learner-centered persuasion, that experience helped make Reese a believer in teacher-centered learning.

Teachers have fond or not-so-fond recollections of their education courses, but there seems to be widespread agreement that the preparatory instruction should have a more practical bent: "I think that student teaching was the most helpful period of my college career," said a teacher in central Pennsylvania (who preferred that her name not be used). "I think pre-service teachers should spend more time in the classroom with a strong mentor teacher, and less time in methods courses. Methods were helpful in learning content, but they really didn't prepare me to teach." Barbara Adams, an elementary teacher in rural northwest Montana, remembers her methods/ materials courses as being "pretty Mickey Mouse," and added that "classroom management classes were nonexistent and definitely needed." Daniel Konieczko, a secondary-school teacher in Maine, concluded that "very few of the courses I took prepared me to handle the challenges of the classroom. . . . The greatest teaching-skill development was found in the classroom," in part with the aid of "daily mentoring from seasoned teachers."

Anyone seriously embarked on a mission to reform schools of education would be well advised to consult with thoughtful teachers like John Szewczyk, a veteran English teacher in the highly regarded Hanover public schools north of Richmond, Virginia. Szewczyk, a leader in a movement to establish an independent professional association of Virginia teachers, firmly believes that professors of education should have "at least five years of public-school teaching experience, preferably with mixed-ability classes and with 'difficult' students. Incredibly, some teacher educators have never set foot in a primary or secondary classroom and can offer their students only theory and hope." Given that classroom conditions can change quickly, Szewczyk adds, it should be imperative that education professors have "current public-school experience." That could take the form of substituting, taking part-time employment in a K–12 school, or participating in a semester exchange program whereby an education professor teaches full-time at a local school. Judy Richardson, an outstanding education professor at Virginia Commonwealth University, is one who has swapped jobs with Jane DeBernardo of Hanover's Patrick Henry High School.

Furthermore, Szewczyk is convinced that education professors "must submit to rigorous post-tenure reviews. I realize that nonproductive instructors can be found in almost every university department, but the results are especially damaging and tragic when teacher trainers fail to prepare college students for the realities of the contemporary public-school classroom." College-level education classes should emphasize practice over theory, given the reality that many first-year teachers are driven out of the profession by "staggering workloads, disruptive students, and endless bureaucratic paperwork." Even simply teaching new teachers how to grade large numbers of essays speedily and correctly could be a major help.

Sara Matthews teaches at an independent school in Pennsylvania, and, like many teachers in private schools, does not have state certification and has taken no education courses. Her academic credentials, however, are impressive: a B.A. in anthropology with a minor in history, and an M.A. and Ph.D. in American Civilization. She has taught with distinction for 20 years at all levels from preschool to college. One might assume Matthews would dismiss the teacher-as-facilitator model so widely advocated in schools of education, but her view is broader than that: "I don't believe there is a 'one size fits all' answer to this good question. I do believe families should be free to choose among schools and that schools should be free to choose among philosophies of education. 'Cookie-cutter' schools serve no one best."

One of the most perceptive critics of education of the past century, Jacques Barzun, once observed that "the way to learn the art of teaching is by imitation. To teach well, one should have had at least one good teacher and been struck, consciously or not, by the means employed and the behavior displayed" (Barzun, 1992: 100). He went on to express fear that in the current climate, with too many teachers misguided by miseducation, imitation would merely produce more of the inadequate classrooms we have now. (Chapter 7 will explore mentoring—an aid to the novice teacher that makes emulation of teaching excellence a possibility.)

Nevertheless, Barzun's idea of "one good teacher" from the past being a model for good teaching in the present has potential. Part of the research for this book entailed asking people from all over the country—some of them active teachers, some not—who was the best teacher they ever had, and why that teacher was so effective. Many of the answers go to the heart of the question "What makes a great teacher?"

Here are some representative responses:

- Candy Steventon, a special educator in public schools for 29 years and currently a doctoral student at Georgia State University:

  My best teacher ever was Mrs. Bertha Spears, my Algebra II high school teacher in a small town in central Florida, Mt. Dora. At the time, I did not think of myself as mathematically astute. I struggled with Algebra I. I grasped geometric concepts quicker than algebraic concepts. My junior year, I entered Mrs. Spears' classroom with a high degree of anxiety. My anxiety level heightened as Mrs. Spears greeted each of us and turned two students away whom she felt were not appropriate for the demands of her class.

  When I attended Mrs. Spears' Algebra II class in fall of 1968, she was in her early 50s, the wife of the head football coach, and mother of three brilliant adult children. Teaching was her profession. She took it seriously.

Mrs. Spears was consistent in her teaching procedures. Her routines were predictable. Review of the previously learned concepts and homework problems, clarification of problem areas, introduction of new concepts, immediate practice of newly learned concepts, and opportunity for corrective feedback were the routines her students came to expect on a daily basis. These teaching routines lessened my anxiety.

Mrs. Spears' stern but quiet demeanor controlled any need for disciplinary actions. She commanded respect by respecting each of us. She was a private person; therefore, she chose to respect our need for privacy. She rarely let her emotions come to the surface. A smile or laugh from her was cherished.

Spring of my junior year, I took the SAT. Surprisingly, my quantitative score was several points higher than my verbal score. I would not have predicted such results.

When I told Mrs. Spears, she smiled.

- Katie Sucato, fourth-grade public-school teacher in the Spring Branch ISD, Houston, Texas:

My favorite teacher was Sister Mary Bernadette, a member of the teaching order of the Sisters of Notre Dame de Namur. I had Sister for Algebra I and Latin I in eighth grade during the 1960–61 school year at Blessed Sacrament School in Norfolk, Virginia. Sister Mary Bernadette was demanding, tough, scary, but patient, and that patience meant everything to providing a solid base in the first years of algebra and Latin. She knew her subjects inside and out and lectured us on a daily basis about the importance of absolutely understanding every facet of what she was teaching. The worst sin one could commit in Sister's classes was pretending to understand a concept. We had daily quizzes, weekly tests, and huge homework assignments. She considered nothing more important than algebra and Latin, and had no sympathy for the fact that we also had homework in other subjects. I don't know whether I ever actually liked Sister. I think I was too afraid of her; however, I respected her tremendously and thanked her in my heart a hundred times over [in] the ensuing years for providing such a strong base and such confidence in my abilities in math and Latin. Both took me far.

- Laura Catherine Dawson Fortune, retired teacher in Evington, Virginia:

My best teacher was Carrie Belle Bowles—later, after marriage, Watts—at Temperance School in Amherst County, Virginia. In the fourth grade in 1939 she taught me many thoughts about Virginian and United States history. I can picture even today the chalk-written unit title, "Transportation and Communication," in which I learned about the covered wagon, the early automobiles, riding a horse, sleds of all kinds, the invention of the telephone and telegraph, smoke signals, talking drums, etc. It was a fascinating unit for me. As a fourth grader, I do not remember, and probably was not even aware of, the methods she used, other than we built some form of transportation (mine was a covered wagon), and we wrote voluminous notes in a notebook in outline form. That was when I learned to outline to remember the important points in any discussion.

I learned after I was an adult that that year was the first year for Carrie Belle to teach. After her marriage, she moved to Richmond and went into the field of social work. After her retirement, she returned to live in Amherst County in the Mount Pleasant community. I saw her several years ago at a Temperance School Grand Reunion. We reminisced about it being the first year in the building, and her class had to be conducted on the stage because there were too many students for the classroom. There were construction problems years ago, too.

As a retired teacher at nearly 71 years of age, I hope that somebody remembers something I did in the classroom as well as I remember what Carrie Belle taught me about the development of transportation and communication in this great country of ours.

- Don Crawford, from Ferndale, Washington, expressed his "best teacher" thoughts in curmudgeonly terms:

Unfortunately, all too often our "best teacher" memories have little to do with whether or not the teacher was an effective teacher. Those teachers who were most attentive, the kindest, the funniest, the sincerest, the most charming, the best-looking, the most inspirational are often fondly remembered and glowingly described. Especially frequently cited are the teachers who introduced us to a new field of thought, new authors, a new discipline, and so on. But the best teachers are the ones who taught us the most content, the ones who raised our test scores the most in a given year and—because we didn't have the benefit of value-added assessment during our schooling—few of us knew who that might be. Sometimes, though rarely, we do focus on those teachers who demanded more than we thought ourselves capable of—and forced us out of our comfort zone. While those experiences are often beneficial, I have often seen the worst teachers (those who are unclear communicators, inadequate reviewers, unfocused lecturers) being the ones who are forced to resort to the pep talk combined with inflexible demands. We seldom can tell just who taught us a great deal of knowledge.

It has long been my opinion that crediting individuals with the appellation of "best teacher" in the absence of any concrete knowledge of how effectively this person taught serves only to perpetuate the myths that methods of teaching are irrelevant—it's just the character or the sincerity of the teacher that counts. Progressive education professors are especially fond of focusing their students on their favorite, or most inspirational, or best teachers as a way of steering away from scientifically effective methods and into the touchy-feely mode of teacher training.

That may be true in some cases. But consider a "best teacher" as recalled by our master of teacher-directed instruction, Donna Garner. Garner recalls her "most wonderful teacher" in the person of Lloyd Huff, who taught her English at McMurry College, Abilene, Texas:

Dr. Huff was the most invigorating individual I have ever known. He always started class about thirty minutes before the official start time; and we students learned that we better be early, too. He had a syllabus for each course; and come rain, sleet, or snow, we stuck with his goals. He exuded energy and life. He loved literature, grammar, and writing; and he made all of those subjects come to life for his students. His high expectations were known by everyone on the campus, and the lazier students lived in fear of being arbitrarily assigned to his classes. We English majors, however, fought to be first in line to register because we knew he was equipping us to be successful English students.

Dr. Huff's advanced grammar class was like unto none. His card file assignment in that class was infamous. We students had to find examples of myriad grammatical elements used either in a Methodist hymnal or in the Bible. (McMurry was a Methodist school.) We searched hour after hour to find those examples, and my card file is still one of my most prized possessions.

At the end of our junior year, we English majors went to see Dr. Huff in order to get set up for our capstone course in literature. He had an extensive reading list filled with the world's greatest classic selections. Using that master list, he designed for each one of us an individualized plan. We started reading right then and kept reading all summer long and throughout the fall semester—thousands and thousands of pages. We kept a literary journal where we documented and discussed each of the assigned books, and that notebook is also a prized possession.

Dr. Lloyd Huff cared enough about each of us to challenge us to go way beyond ourselves. He had the expertise and the credentials to teach in any large university in the United States or in England, but he chose to rear his family in a small-town setting and teach in small colleges. I have talked to many of his graduates through the years, and we all have the same testimony: We could not have been successful in our fields had it not been for Dr. Huff's marvelous training.

Not surprisingly, when Donna Garner and other Texas classroom teachers concluded in 1996–1997 that they needed to write their own

English/Language Arts/Reading curriculum standards because of the innocuous document being produced by the Texas Education Agency, Huff and his wife (also a superb professor) spent countless hours helping them build the Texas Alternative Document (TAD), pre-K through grade 12. The TAD has been acclaimed by many education experts and by the general public because of its high, clearly stated academic expectations—largely due, notes Garner, to the input from the Huffs.

So the debate about the nature of effective teaching rages, as it always has and forever will. Is the proof of good teaching based on the empirical or the inspirational? Should the evidence of a teacher's impact be rigorously scientific or at least partly based on the intangible, even the sentimental? Results count for much—but what results, and how will they be measured? A great teacher should have a passion for his or her branch of learning and a tireless inner drive to impart that enthusiasm to his or her students (Stephenson, 2001). Beyond that, noted the great academic Jacques Barzun, the master teacher should have lively interests beyond his or her specialty. The teacher should exude the "spontaneous mental radiation" of a person with a genuine intellectual life, one who reads books and converses about substance rather than just prattling about methods and process (Barzun, 1992).

The crucial question is whether America's highly regulated and bureaucratic system of teacher preparation and licensing is up to the task of building that kind of teacher.

# CHAPTER 3

## Data Define the Problem

This is not a book about statistics; it is a book about teaching. However, to understand the challenges that teachers and families alike face in turning around American education, it is useful to look at indicators of achievement.

Granted, numbers don't always tell the whole story. Moreover, spin doctors can use numbers selectively to render a misleading account. When confronted by advocates bearing statistics, it is usually prudent to remember the statistician who drowned in water that averaged three feet in depth.

Cassandras and Pollyannas perpetually bicker over the education numbers. The gloomsters paint a picture of education decline so bleak as to invite despair. Chirpy apologists for the K–12 school system contend comparisons are unfair because of the growing demographic diversity of American schools and the breakup of the traditional family, as well as the belief that the U.S. public schools generally do not deliberately weed out difficult-to-teach children.

The truth lies not entirely on one side or the other. However, when viewed as a whole, data about the condition of American education do suggest the need for sober reflection on what we can do to make our schools places where teachers can effectively instruct a broad range of children from widely varied backgrounds.

Part of our common task must be attracting bright, motivated persons to the job of K–12 teaching, and another part must be rewarding and retaining those who do a good job helping children learn.

Three of the scariest numbers circulating in the education world in recent years are these:

- *Two million, two hundred thousand (2.2 million)*. That's approximately the number of new teaching hires said to be needed by 2010 just to maintain the status quo.
- *Fifty-nine (59) percent*. That's the proportion of prospective teachers in Massachusetts schools of education who flunked a basic competency test in 1998. Only two-thirds were able to pass the literacy portion of the exam. If that happened in the sophisticated Bay State, it is reasonable to assume that literacy testing in other states would reveal not dissimilar results.
- *Thirty-nine (39) percent*. That's the percentage of teachers who have left teaching five years after starting. (Ingersoll, 2001)

Some of those numbers are scarier than others. For instance, the challenge of finding additional teachers often gets hyped as a crisis-level "teacher shortage." "Shortage" may accurately describe the situation in fields where teacher salaries are less than competitive, such as mathematics and science. But analysts dealing in facts and offering a calmer perspective note that many such vacancies typically are filled by ex-teachers returning to the profession, or teachers transferring from one district to another, or teachers moving from private schools to public schools (Feistritzer, 1999). A prominent University of Pennsylvania researcher has argued that those concerned with the teacher shortage ought to focus instead on reducing teacher turnover, particularly among teachers in their first five years in the classroom. He states that school systems could accomplish that by improving teacher pay and working conditions (Ingersoll, 2001). Be that as it may, the 2.2 million figure may furnish more of a reason to be excited about the possibility of change than to be frightened at the prospect.

Another kind of alarming number is the rather consistent pattern of education majors ranking at or near the bottom when the SAT scores of entering undergraduates are compared by major field of study. That's a legitimate source of concern, but such figures shouldn't be used to taint teachers as a group. Group averages do not apply to all individuals, nor do SAT scores correlate with the ability to teach or with dedication to helping children. But if the averages indicate many of the brightest college students are shunning teaching as a career, that's a legitimate concern.

A broader view would examine the condition of education as a whole, and regard raising quality as a shared responsibility. In 1983, the famous *A Nation at Risk* report that the National Commission on Excellence in Education issued in concert with the Reagan administration invoked martial rhetoric. "If an unfriendly foreign power had attempted to impose on America the mediocre educational performance that exists today," the Commission asserted, "we might well have viewed it as an act of war." In support of its conclusions, the panel served up a depressing litany of national "risk," including declining SAT scores from 1963 to 1980, poor showings in international comparisons of academic prowess, and high levels of functional illiteracy, particularly among minority youth (National Commission, 1983).

The dire warnings set the stage for the crusade to establish and enforce standards in education that continues to this day. To be sure, many defenders of the system pooh-poohed the rhetoric and even saw it as a conspiracy to "manufacture a crisis" (Berliner and Biddle, 1995). There can be legitimate debate over how data are interpreted—for instance, the SAT was never meant to be a report card on schools and school districts.

Nevertheless, in 2001 the appalling events of September 11—when viewed together with more recent indicators of educational quality—made the martial rhetoric freshly pertinent.

Suddenly the phrase du jour was "homeland defense." That has to mean more than gathering accurate intelligence, securing the borders, and demolishing terrorist cells. It also has to mean educating a new generation so its members can read, do math, understand science, and generally become astute citizens who will strive to keep the nation vibrant (Holland, 2002). At those critical tasks, a whole mass of recent data from official and private sources alike shows American schools are not performing as well as needed to secure the nation's future.

Counting money by all levels of government, Americans spend more tax money on education than on national defense. Only Social Security consumes more dollars than local, state, and federal governments spend on the schools. Since the 1960s, reports the Institute for Policy Innovation, the number of pupils per teacher has fallen 32 percent, while the number of teachers holding advanced degrees has doubled. Waves of so-called reform have brought a sharp rise in school spending and the nationally ballyhooed "standards" (Franciosi, 2001).

Yet, just before Thanksgiving 2001, the National Assessment of Educational Progress (NAEP), also known as the Nation's Report Card, brought the unpleasant tidings that high school seniors who had been tested in 2000 actually knew *less* about science than did high school seniors who were tested in 1996. The drop was not huge—

three points on a test scored on a 0–300 scale; however, it indicated that the country has not exactly been roaring ahead toward the "first in the world in math and science" National Goal that Congress wrote into law in 1994 as part of the Clinton administration's Goals 2000 (NCES, 2001c). Today those National Goals have been shoved to the background because of embarrassment (and partly the concern that setting goals for schools is not really the function of the federal government). The National Education Goals Panel has passed out of existence. Alas, in science and math, U.S. students perform closer to the bottom of the world's industrialized nations than to the top. And as for closing the much-lamented "achievement gap" between whites and blacks—an objective for which the federal government has shelled out $130 billion since the mid-1960s—the report showed only a perverse sort of narrowing. While the science scores of white seniors fell from 159 to 154, the scores of blacks declined just one point—from 124 to 123. In short, the gap narrowed slightly, but only because the scores of whites were declining faster than those of blacks (Holland, 2002).

Overall, on the latest NAEP for science, only 18 percent of high school seniors scored at or above "proficient," the level connoting solid academic performance. Almost half failed to reach even a "basic" level. That stands for only partial, inadequate mastery of the subject. It is not synonymous with "adequate."

Fourth and eighth graders performed a bit better: 29 percent of grade 4 and 32 percent of grade 8 were at or above "proficient." However, that only underscored a perverse phenomenon exposed by other recent national and international comparisons—the longer American kids stay in the public schools, the more their achievement lags.

U.S. Secretary of Education Rod Paige, a former Houston school superintendent, didn't try to deny the seriousness of the situation. "The decline is not huge," he said, "but it is statistically significant and morally significant as well. After all, 12th-grade scores are the scores that really matter. If our graduates know less about science than their predecessors four years ago, then our hopes for a strong 21st-century workforce are dimming just when we need them the most."

In a report anticipating this and other bad news, the U.S. Commission on National Security/21st Century recognized in a February 15, 2001, report both the threat of a sneak terrorist attack (such as occurred on the Pentagon and World Trade Center seven months later) and the part that a troubled public-school system may play in the erosion of national security unless its decline is reversed.

Headed by former U.S. Senators Warren Rudman and Gary Hart, the commission recommended formation of a National Homeland Security Agency (along the lines of what President Bush finally proposed in June 2002) as well as the rebuilding of national leadership in research and K–12 education. The commission recognized that national security and a sound education system are inseparable. Noting that many corporations had cited a severe shortage of technically skilled Americans as a rationale for importing such help from overseas via special H-1B visas, the commission warned that "large numbers of specialized foreign technicians in critical positions in the U.S. economy could pose security risks" (Rudman and Hart, 2001).

The same commission had warned in its first report, in September 1999, that "we should expect conflicts in which adversaries, because of cultural affinities different from our own, will resort to forms and levels of violence shocking to our sensibilities." The 14-member body proved eerily prophetic in warning that "Americans will likely die on American soil, possibly in large numbers" (Rudman and Hart, 1999).

The September 11, 2001, terrorist atrocity underscored the need for rising generations of Americans to understand their own nation's heritage and values, given that it will be they who will defend the nation's very existence, if it is to be defended. Yet, in May 2002 came the results of a national assessment showing that high school seniors were as woefully deficient in an understanding of U.S. history as they had been in the last such assessment seven years earlier. Overall, almost six of every ten students tested could not demonstrate even a rock-bottom "basic" knowledge of history, according to NAEP. "The questions that stumped so many students," lamented Secretary Paige, "involve the most fundamental concepts of our democracy, our growth as a nation, and our role in the world" (Manzo, 2002: 1, 15).

Some educators attributed students' poor showing in history to that subject's being slighted in favor of emphasis on mathematics and sciences. Unfortunately, the Third International Mathematics and Science Study (TIMSS) has exposed mediocre performance by U.S. students in those critical subjects as well. U.S. education officials thought they saw a ray of hope in the original TIMSS scores in 1995, although the scores of U.S. eighth graders were below average and marks for the U.S. twelfth graders were among the lowest in the entire world. U.S. fourth graders actually scored above average in science and about average in math (Holland, 2001).

Believing this meant the highly touted "standards-based reform" promoted by Washington was kicking in and would be sustained,

American officials asked for a TIMMS-Repeat in 1999 to examine scores just for eighth graders. They hoped 1995's fourth graders would continue to shine as eighth graders. Thirty-eight nations participated in TIMMS-R.

Alas, mediocrity prevailed again. Released in late 2000, the TIMMS-R data showed that the current eighth graders did far worse on science than had the fourth graders of four years earlier, plummeting from third place among participating nations all the way down to nineteenth. In math, the scores slid from twelfth to eighteenth place (TIMSS-R, 2001).

The results exposed once again the raw reality that the longer children stay in government-run schools in the United States, the worse they perform when measured by objective tests.

Recent NAEP reports on reading and math have brought no better news. According to NAEP year 2000 data, two-thirds of U.S. fourth graders score less than "proficient" in reading. And in the 2000 NAEP for math, scores for fourth graders were up from 1996 and 1990 but, again, scores for high school seniors fell (NCES, 2001b).

In December 2001, a study by the Paris-based Organization for Economic Cooperation and Development (OECD) of 15-year-olds in 32 industrialized nations found that American students achieved only an average level score when their ability to use science, math, and reading skills in "real-life" applications was gauged. Only Mexico, Greece, Portugal, and Luxembourg scored below the United States in science (Schemo, 2001).

An even more ominous OECD report was published in the spring of 2001. It concluded that extremely poor literacy skills among U.S. high school graduates threaten to cost the United States its competitive edge. OECD's concern for the fate of a free market may be suspect, but its statistics on literacy are revealing nonetheless.

Among 18 industrialized nations, OECD found that the United States ranked dead last in the literacy of 16-to-25-year-old high school graduates who did not go on to further educational studies. Almost 60 percent of the U.S. graduates performed below a level considered minimally necessary to deal with "the complex demands of modern life." Finland ranked first, with only 10 percent lacking in literacy.

In 1970, said an OECD official, the United States was the "undisputed leader" in educating its people. Now it is being passed like a horse-and-buggy that wandered on the freeway (Gehring, 2001).

One indication that American schools once did a much better job of educating the populace is that the United States led all the countries in high school completion rates among 50-to-54-year-olds. But those rates have been plummeting lately. Recently Manhattan Institute scholar Jay P. Greene computed a national graduation rate for the class of 1998 of 74 percent. He established clearly that the rate of 86 percent reported by the federal government is inflated by misleading data turned in by local schools that fail to account for many dropouts.

Furthermore, in a study done for the Black Alliance for Educational Options, Greene found that many of the nation's urban school districts have graduation rates that can only be described as catastrophic. Cleveland was the worst, with only 28 percent of 1993's eighth graders graduating five years later (Greene, 2001). Cleveland public schools also had the distinction recently of flunking 18 out of 18 state achievement tests. With that report card in mind, a decision issued June 27, 2002, by a 5–4 U.S. Supreme Court majority upheld the constitutionality of Ohio's experimental voucher program enabling at least a few thousand needy children to escape Cleveland's woeful public schools for private, primarily religious ones (*Zelman* v. *Simmons-Harris,* 2002).

The contrast between America's growing private economy and the stagnant public schools has provoked acerbic comment, such as the following: "We invent the Internet, create breakthrough technologies, learn how to treat illnesses in creative new ways, manufacture ever-improving consumer goods. . . . [Yet,] American school children regularly lag behind international competitions. Millions of children— particularly minorities—are forced to attend schools that don't even teach them to read effectively, much less become well-educated members of society" (Von Kohorn, 2002: 39). True, it may be argued that graduates of the school system helped produce the economic bounty, but as Connecticut education activist and author Ken Von Kohorn points out, there is a strong anticompetitive spirit in today's schools that threatens to waste the productive potential of future adults. Indicative of this mind-set is the growing refusal to recognize true meritorious achievement of individuals. Grade inflation has made yesterday's "C" today's "A," and honor rolls resemble small-town telephone directories. Increasingly schools are nixing the tradition of naming the top-ranked student the class valedictorian. Now, in an egalitarian fashion, that honor can be shared by dozens.

Increases in productivity have been crucial to American economic progress. How does productivity in public education compare? George

A. Clowes, managing editor of *School Reform News*, noted that labor productivity rises with one or more of the following production changes: a larger quantity of an unchanged quality output; the same quantity of a higher-quality output; fewer rejects. Since 1970, the Bureau of Labor Statistics shows a 74 percent increase in U.S. worker productivity. If economists applied the same model to schools, labor productivity would rise over time if schools produced a larger quantity of graduates of the same quality, an unchanged quantity of higher-quality graduates, or fewer nongraduates.

After weighing NAEP data such as that cited earlier, Clowes pointed out that the pupil/teacher ratio in public schools declined from 22.3 in 1970 to 14.1 in 1999, a drop of 27.4 percent. Coupled with the stagnant student achievement, the reduced pupil/teacher ratio indicates that K–12 public education has become significantly less productive over the past three decades. "In 1999," noted Clowes, "public schools require half as many staff in total (up 58.1 percent)—including a third more teachers (up 37.6 percent)—to educate the same number of children to the same level of quality as they did in 1970. Thus, while productivity in the economy as a whole increased by 74 percent, productivity in K–12 education fell by 27 percent" (Clowes, 2002).

Defenders of the system would respond that working with children is not like manufacturing furniture. There are many intangibles, and family factors largely beyond the control of the school create snafus in production of a kind not typically faced by manufacturers. There is some truth in that, but nevertheless it is reasonable to hold education to bottom-line outcomes because of its social value in both human and economic terms.

Within recent years a study by the Milton and Rose D. Friedman Foundation offered another way to look at the efficiency of the educational system. Drawing on data from massive government studies of illiteracy as well as reports of school expenditures, foundation researchers developed an index to measure literacy as the bottom-line outcome of education (Holland and Soifer, 2000). They found that public schools in the 50 states and the District of Columbia were wasting from 13 to 23 percent of the tax money to the extent that they were failing at their most fundamental job: ensuring that all students can read and write at a basic level. Given that limited additional learning can occur without the ability to read, it seems reasonable to measure public education by a literacy yardstick.

The Friedman researchers used the U.S. Department of Education's seminal study issued in 1993, *Adult Literacy in America*, which categorized literacy as three types (prose, document, and quantitative) and measured from Level I (the lowest) to Level V. In calculating waste in the educational process, the researchers used Level I and II data for students still in high school and high school graduates who had not received additional formal education. They used expenditure data for the 1995–1996 school year as provided in the 1998 *Digest of Education Statistics* published by the National Center for Education Statistics. They deemed their calculations of waste conservative, given that they did not attempt to include dropouts. In addition, it is possible that some high school graduates counted in the study may have gained literacy skills from remedial tutoring after leaving school. That would make the schools' performance appear a bit better than it actually was.

According to a 1998 government report, *The State of Literacy in America*, persons at Level I literacy "cannot usually perform" such functions as finding an intersection on a street map or entering background information on a Social Security application. Level II folks were only marginally more functional. It would not seem a lot to ask that public schools raise the majority of Americans above these two pitiable levels. Yet almost half of adult Americans fall into one of those two categories, and literacy skills for persons in their early twenties actually were lower than had been the case a decade earlier, in 1985.

By means of a formula to calculate money wasted from failure to achieve basic literacy, the Friedman study found that U.S. public schools frittered away a staggering $49.2 billion in a recent year. The three population giants—California, New York, and Texas—wasted 18 percent of their expenditures. The highest rate of waste was the District of Columbia, at 23 percent, followed by Mississippi, 21 percent; Louisiana, 20 percent; and Alabama, Florida, and South Carolina, 19 percent. Just behind the population giants, at 17 percent, were Arkansas, Illinois, Maryland, New Jersey, New Mexico, North Carolina, Tennessee, and West Virginia.

Some critics will note that the low literacy closely corresponds to high levels of poverty and concentrations of minority population. Certainly, it is true that *Adult Literacy in America* found that more than 40 percent of persons at the lowest levels of literacy met the federal poverty guidelines, and that African-Americans and Hispanics were more likely than whites to score low on literacy scales. However, as the study argued, it is wrong to use socioeconomic data as a defeatist excuse. Failure to teach reading is failure to teach reading—and to make excuses is to imprison children by resorting to what George W. Bush has called "the soft bigotry of low expectations." Besides, some citizens may be in poverty in part because their schools failed to teach them the common language needed for landing a good job. Furthermore, a cottage industry has grown up around a misnamed brand of bilingual education that keeps immigrant children functioning in their native language for as long as eight years before even attempting to teach them English. (Fortunately, a reform movement that includes many Hispanic parents is becoming increasingly successful in shortening the bilingual transition in favor of prompt English mastery.)

It does no favor to disadvantaged children to imply that they should be held to lower standards than mainstream students. To lower expectations of achievement for some students because of the size of their family's bank account or the color of their skin is to engage in a self-fulfilling prophecy that denies equal opportunity. There is value in using an absolute standard, such as the Friedman waste index, that assumes all children will be taught the basics of literacy. Indeed, the landmark report of the National Reading Panel, a congressionally mandated study coordinated by the National Institute of Child Health and Human Development, established that children can be taught to read if schools use scientifically proven approaches that stress phonemic awareness, phonics, fluency, vocabulary, and text comprehension.

Furthermore, the record shows that holding so-called at-risk children to high standards is perfectly reasonable. It is doable. With the proper motivation and instruction, they can rise to the challenge. The American public should not tolerate high levels of illiteracy/waste as a normal by-product of public education.

Recognition that high-poverty schools can also be high-achievement schools has come from across the political spectrum. A 1999 study for the Heritage Foundation by Samuel Casey Carter introduced the nation to "No Excuses" schools. Carter visited and wrote about schools in the poorest sections of Chicago, Detroit, Houston, Los Angeles, and New York where principals simply would not tolerate low achievement—and therefore students achieved; they succeeded (Carter, 2000).

Carter reported that in 1974, when Nancy Ichinaga became principal of Los Angeles' Andrew Bennett (now Bennett-Kew) Elementary, an appalling 95 percent of pupils there were illiterate. Within four years, the reading level of the school's pupils had risen from the third to the fiftieth percentile in California, and by the time Carter visited in 1999, the school's reading scores had risen to among the highest in Los Angeles County. How could this happen? "One of our most successful interventions," Ichinaga told Carter, "has been to require kindergartners to know all the letter sounds and to be able to blend three letters to read words."

From his visit to the Big Apple, Carter found that even though 98 percent of pupils at Brooklyn's P.S. 161 met poverty guidelines for free or reduced-price lunch, the school's sixth graders had the second-highest reading scores in New York State. Moreover, in Harlem, he found that at the Frederick Douglass Academy, 80 percent of students met the poverty guidelines, and the enrollment is 79 percent black and 20 percent Hispanic. Yet the Academy's pupils required no excuses because they were topping the New York City average by 32 percentage points in reading.

Meanwhile, the Education Trust, a liberal-oriented school reform organization, has done its own research that shows the "No Excuses" schools are not just isolated exceptions. The Trust identified more than 4,500 high-poverty and/or high-minority schools nationwide that scored in the top one-third of all schools in their states. The data for 2000, the latest year for which data were available from every state, do not reflect improvement, because they are for one year only. However, over time, this database could become ever more useful in identifying high-achieving schools generating little waste, despite the predominance of socioeconomic backgrounds that apologists for public schools deem insurmountable barriers to achievement.

The Education Trust's project features a searchable database (www.edtrust.org) that parents, policymakers, school reformers, and journalists can use to identify schools according to whatever performance and socioeconomic data the searcher specifies.

In sum, there is good news despite the succession of reports filled with dreary statistics about the condition of education.

As 2001 was ending, the House of Representatives and Senate joined in a bipartisan fashion to pass the No Child Left Behind Act, an education reform sought as a high priority by President George W. Bush, who now leads the nation in a war against terrorism. The reauthorized Elementary and Secondary Education Act (ESEA) seeks to impose accountability by requiring states to administer reading and math tests to all students in grades 3–8 every year. When schools fail to make sufficient progress, they could be converted to charter schools or parents could use their federal subsidies of $500 to $1,000 per child to purchase remedial help from private providers, such as tutorial services. In addition, the new ESEA seeks to bust the linguistic ghettos spawned by so-called bilingual education by requiring the teaching of English to students whose native language is not English.

A big question mark hangs over these latest federal initiatives in education. Critics have made a strong case that American education declined in quality the more the federal bureaucracy intervened in K–12 policy during the decades since the passage of the original ESEA under Lyndon Johnson in 1965. Governmental clout is a must in combating terrorism, but even though quality of education is critical for securing the nation's future, considerable doubt exists that directives from Washington can transform educational mediocrity into educational excellence. That is more properly a task for parents, teachers, and students in communities across the country. However, federal policies may be able to nudge local and state policies in the direction of real reform. As will be noted in later chapters, in no area does the No Child Left Behind Act make a greater effort to do that than in teacher quality. The new program gives states and localities flexibility to speed career-switchers' transition to teaching jobs, to give bonuses to teachers in high-need subjects such as mathematics and science, and to award merit pay to teachers who help their students make significant improvements.

By putting the emphasis on adding value to education through attracting and retaining superior teachers, the new approach could make statistics about educational performance in the United States far brighter.

# CHAPTER 4

# *The Certification Mill*

American schools need to hire great numbers of teachers. The number incessantly repeated is more than 2 million over the next decade. But schools especially need *better* teachers. Teacher shortages come and go, but schools never seem to enjoy surpluses of excellent teachers. Unfortunately, the public regulation of teacher training and licensure appears to have been more effective in preserving the education establishment's tight control over the teaching profession than it has been in delivering high-quality teaching in quantity to the classrooms.

State departments of education and the collegiate schools of education act as the gatekeepers to teaching. Rather than serving as regulators who look after the public interest, the state education bureaucracies collaborate with the education schools to use government power to standardize and centralize teacher education—a relationship economists describe as "regulatory capture" (Stone, 1999). Since the early decades of the twentieth century, learned critics have hammered away at an exercise of power that excludes—rather than welcomes— liberally educated persons into the world of teaching. At midcentury, Arthur Bestor, a professor emeritus of history at the University of Washington, delivered perhaps the most withering criticism, terming the controllers of teacher preparation and licensure an "interlocking directorate of professional educationists" (Bestor, 1953).

The iron-fisted control was a twentieth-century phenomenon that persists into the twenty-first despite the spectacular success of free markets in other human activities. Throughout the nineteenth century, control was distinctly local, not centralized. Local school authorities usually administered an examination to aspiring teachers, who did not have to show that they had taken several semesters' worth of courses in pedagogy. As school systems grew much larger and America began urbanizing, that changed drastically during the first three decades of the twentieth century. Education historian David Angus found that intellectual sophisticates began to deem teacher examinations by lay boards of education (the common practice in rural America) to be hopelessly provincial (Angus and Mirel, 2001). In the place of such direct hiring came bureaucratic education specialists to mull over candidates' transcripts and vitae. Teachers colleges emerged to provide the specialized training or pedagogy thought essential for all who would teach in the public schools (which, of course, became much less public as control slipped from local boards to a faceless establishment).

As this system took hold, leadership of the education profession fell to those who had garnered the requisite credentials in education school. The system became largely self-perpetuating and fiercely dedicated to the status quo as education graduates took command of school districts and education associations, and enforced requirements that newcomers be steeped in pedagogy to the same degree that they had been. Outsiders with fresh perspectives need not apply.

An "education trust" is how Angus characterized the school superintendents, state education officials, national and state association leaders, and federal paper-pushers who controlled the gates to teaching with minimal regard for wishes of parents and other taxpayers. A more acerbic critic during the 1960s—James D. Koerner—termed the collaborationists an Establishment, and observed that it dominated professional education. Its major components were the state departments of education, accrediting associations, professional associations (which have since evolved into the two teacher unions, the NEA and AFT), and the teacher-training institutions. He found all of these elements to be "complementing and reinforcing one another and all staffed by persons who are themselves graduates of the advanced training programs in education and who share the same basic educational views" (Koerner, 1963).

Almost 40 years later, critics assail in much the same terms the inbred, elitist nature of control over entrance to K–12 teaching. Here's how one critic of the education establishment's notion of reform put it: "In the name of 'professionalizing' the teaching field, a well-organized cadre of national teacher education groups—working in close cooperation with the two major teacher unions—seeks to transfer authority over teacher training and certification away from states and localities to private managerial agencies. These agencies are run by the cadre's own members, who stand to gain much from a centralized teacher education system under their control and unaccountable to the public" (Policy Brief, 2001: 4). As a French philosopher once observed, *Plus ca change, plus c'est la meme chose*—"The more things change, the more they stay the same."

In the post–World War II era, a chorus of critics led by university arts and sciences professors denounced schools of education for offering intellectually shallow courses (dubbed "Mickey Mouse" for their inanity) and education bureaucracies for imposing such dubious pedagogy on would-be teachers. But wave after wave of reform commissions did little more than shuffle the players in the power elite a little; the trust stayed intact and, if anything, only increased in power with each passing effort at reform.

Although teacher licensing requirements vary from one state to another, all 50 states require new teachers to hold a bachelor's degree and to have completed a specified number of pedagogical or how-to-teach courses in order to be fully certified (Ballou and Podgursky, 1999). Some states require that the degree be earned in professional education, while others accept a major in an academic discipline such as English or mathematics. Some that permit an undergraduate academic major expect would-be teachers to acquire a master's degree in education thereafter. The one constant is that the states expect a significant load of education courses in the mix, as well as practice teaching, which together can consume well over a year of college. In addition, most states require prospective teachers to pass one or more tests of subject-area or pedagogical knowledge, or simple basic skills. As noted in chapter 3, Massachusetts provided a wake-up call to the nation a few years ago when it reported that 59 percent of its candidate teachers had flunked a simple test of literacy.

The states' array of certificates and endorsements can be bewilderingly complex. For instance, Missouri awards certificates to suitably credentialed candidates in 73 subject-matter and 119 vocational areas. A pair of economists who have extensively investigated the system say that Missouri is merely "a typical state in this regard" (Ballou and Podgursky, 1999). No wonder teachers forever are being classified as uncertified and admonished to go back to education schools in the evenings and summers to take new course work to upgrade their certificates.

The critical question for education reform is whether all of these required courses in professional education contribute in any significant way to the quality of teaching in U.S. schools. Studies have shown convincingly that effective teaching greatly improves children's chances of success with their academic lessons. But considerable doubt exists that a mass of required education courses makes teachers more effective in the classroom.

Dozens of reports and rebuttals have debated that point over the years, but the sharpest division of opinion may have come from release of a study late in 2001 by the Baltimore-based Abell Foundation (Walsh, 2001), followed by a blistering retort from perhaps the nation's number one defender of mandatory credentialing of teachers via the schools of pedagogy (Darling-Hammond, 2001).

Outside Baltimore, the exchange received scant media attention. Therefore, a close examination of these dueling reports provides a way to clarify what certification is all about and whether it should be reformed or just terminated.

Written by senior policy analyst Kate Walsh, the Abell study (titled *Teacher Certification Reconsidered: Stumbling for Quality*) purported to analyze from the past 50 years more than 200 studies that mandatory certification advocates have used to claim that certified teachers are more effective than teachers who are not certified. In general, Abell found these studies to be of "astonishingly poor quality," and far from meeting basic standards for scientific research. These were some of the specific criticisms of the certification studies:

- Research receiving no peer review, and relying heavily on unpublished dissertations, was given undeserved weight.
- Rather than use standardized measures of student achievement, advocates simply designed their own, subjective measures to assert certification's value.
- Reports were padded with multiple references that appeared to lend support to certification but, once actually read, did not.
- Much research was too old to be retrieved or to be reliable.
- The researchers routinely violated principles of sound statistical analysis— e.g., by failing to control for such key variables as poverty and prior student achievement.

Abell said it found a contrasting body of scientifically sound research, conducted primarily by economists and social scientists, that defined the attributes of effective teachers. Those studies showed that the best teachers actually were to be found outside the domain of schools of education and compulsory certification. The single attribute found to be most consistently related to a teacher's success in raising student achievement was the teacher's verbal ability. That was consistent with findings that teachers who have graduated from selective universities are most likely to elevate student achievement.

Maryland's Department of Education cited 12 studies, newsletters, and articles as bolstering the legitimacy of its complex system of certification (not unlike other states, Maryland offers 66 different kinds of teaching certificates in its regulation). However, Abell found that only three of those documents even attempted to link teacher certification to higher student achievement, and none did so convincingly. In 1990, in a burst of reform, Maryland inaugurated an alternative route to the classroom called the Resident Teacher Certificate for well-prepared noneducation majors, and also slashed the education course work required for regular certification. But Abell found that in the late 1990s the state largely diluted these reforms by adding new education course work, ostensibly to support a new initiative for the teaching of reading. Because of regulatory obstacles and hostility from the education establishment, the Resident alternative has provided only 500 new teachers out of 50,000 hired in the state since 1990.

Abell's recommendations were aimed at Maryland, which is within its policy orbit, but clearly they could apply to the government-run certification mills of all 50 states:

1. Eliminate course work requirements for teacher certification in favor of simpler and more flexible rules. The only fixed requirement would be a bachelor's degree and a passing score on an appropriate teacher's exam, especially one indicating the teacher's verbal ability. The elementary teacher would have to demonstrate a knowledge of particular skills, such as research-based reading instruction, and the secondary teacher would have to show a grasp of necessary specialized knowledge of the subject to be taught.
2. In the interest of accountability, report the average verbal ability scores of teachers in each district and of teacher candidates graduating from the schools of education.

3. Devolve responsibility for teacher qualifications and selection from the state bureaucracy to the 24 school districts, and encourage those districts in turn to place responsibility for hiring primarily in the hands of principals.
4. At the local level, devise more productive ways for teachers to gain instructional skills and knowledge on the job. Reduce first-year teaching loads, expand in-school training aligned with the curriculum, and evaluate teachers on the basis of demonstrated results.

Walsh concluded that such an overhaul would constitute "a direct threat to schools of education and other education groups that benefit from the flawed certification process." Although these groups typically concede that teacher preparation needs improvement, "their reform agenda consistently leads to heavier state regulation, more time for prospective teachers in schools of education, and a crackdown on alternative certification routes and waivers. It is patently insufficient to consider another re-tooling of the certification process. Reinvention is in order" (Walsh, 2001: 8, 9).

Although this report was relevant to the national debate, Abell is a foundation dedicated to improving the quality of life in Baltimore and throughout Maryland. Its recommendations were directed specifically at the Maryland Department of Education. Nonetheless, the national education establishment took the criticism personally. A stern attack on the report came almost instantaneously from the leading spokesman for tightly controlled teacher certification—Stanford University professor of education Linda Darling-Hammond, the founding Executive Director of the National Commission on Teaching and America's Future (NCTAF), the body bankrolled by two of the highly elite foundations, Carnegie and Rockefeller.

On the very day (October 8, 2001) the Abell Foundation released its study, NCTAF had a press release on its Web site proclaiming that it had "refuted" the Abell report and quoting Darling-Hammond and other panjandrums of the education establishment at length (NCTAF, 2001). Just a week after the report's release, Darling-Hammond's full 69-page response—lengthier by a third than the main text of the report being critiqued—was on the NCTAF Web site (Darling-Hammond, 2001). This exercise in thin-skinned overkill brought to mind yet another astute observation by Arthur Bestor in 1953, in *Educational Wastelands*. Whenever a whisper of criticism comes from outside the educationist circles, he said, there is a "closing of the ranks" symptomatic of the reality that "independence of thought has ceased to be a virtue among professional educationists." Bestor said this monolithic resistance to criticism suggests there is a "party line that protects the vested interests of both school administrators and professors of education." The resolute unwillingness to accept honest criticism frequently assumes the ugly form of showering critics with "vituperation and personal abuse," Bestor noted.

Darling-Hammond did not stoop to name-calling, but she had nothing but ill to say of Kate Walsh's effort to take an in-depth look at the research supposedly underpinning teacher certification. "A stunning exercise in misrepresentation" was the first description of Walsh's work from the Darling-Hammond pen, and her treatment of the critic got no softer thereafter. She repeatedly stated that Walsh had an "agenda," thus implying that Walsh bent her analysis to fit predetermined conclusions. Of course, the national commission Darling-Hammond has led has its own rather sweeping agenda to make certification even more controlling, as will be seen in the next chapter.

The disagreements between Walsh the critic and Darling-Hammond the defender of the teacher-education monopoly boil down to 19 studies that Darling-Hammond cites to demonstrate the value of teacher certification (as opposed to the 200 she had lauded in some of her previous writings). Quibbling over the technical details of such studies could go on endlessly. But the studies in question seem weak reeds on which to prop a monopoly. Arguing that more teacher education is always better than less, Darling-Hammond seeks to make the point by asserting that teachers who complete five-year progams are "more effective" than those who go through traditional four-year programs. But neither of the two studies she cited used student achievement as the measure of teacher effectiveness. That is a common blind spot of apologists for the certification mill.

Furthermore, Abell is not alone in citing the deficiency of research on this subject. A report by the University of Washington Center for the Study of Teaching and Policy reached essentially the same conclusion: "There is no research that directly assesses what teachers learn in their pedagogical preparation and then evaluates the relationship of that pedagogical knowledge to student learning or teacher behavior." Furthermore, a group of scholars organized as the Education Consumers Clearinghouse Consultants Network suggested, in concurring with Abell's basic findings, that another kind of evidence be considered: the utter failure of teacher certification to protect the public from unsound and ineffective practices in education.

"Professor Darling-Hammond may argue about the teacher certification literature but the larger conclusion is reasonably evident," said these education scholars in a statement. "If the kind of standards recommended by the education community were an effective means of ensuring teacher quality, the many rewrites of accreditation and certification standards over the past 50 years would have reduced the use of faddish innovation and increased the use of proven practice. Instead, the opposite has taken place. Highly controversial practices such as Whole Language reading instruction have been widely adopted and well-tested methodologies like Direct Instruction have been rejected on the grounds that they infringe on teacher creativity" (ECC Consultants, 2001).

Indeed, one of the most intriguing of Darling-Hammond's criticisms was that in insinuating that teachers do not need specialized instruction in how to teach, the Abell report had ignored the research findings of the National Reading Panel of the National Institute of Child Health and Human Development. In a well-documented study, the Panel confirmed that the systematic teaching of phonemic awareness (phonemes being the basic units of speech that correspond to the letters of an alphabetic writing system) is essential in beginning reading instruction and urged that teachers be trained to teach phonics as well as the skills of comprehension. Darling-Hammond's point was that teachers of reading need preservice training in schools of education to teach effectively—which would be a telling point indeed if schools of education actually taught teachers how to teach phonics. To the contrary, despite the accumulation of evidence as to how vital phonetic decoding skills are to learning how to read, the vast majority of education professors maintain an ideological hard line against phonics, much preferring the constructivist mind-set of Whole Language, which holds that children will read in their own good time and by their own inclination if only they are surrounded by good books. A survey of the nation's teacher training institutions in the mid-1990s found that shockingly few teacher candidates (including those who would become teachers of reading) received an adequate grounding in phonemic awareness, the speech-sound system, and how our orthography represents spoken English (Moats, 1995). The sad truth is that many principals have to retrain certified reading teachers who weren't taught scientifically valid reading methods in education school. It might well be more efficient if the training were done correctly at the school level, on the job, in summer institutes, or with the help of experienced teachers, rather than relying on the doctrine-driven professional schools of education.

If the blizzard of statements, refutations, and rejoinders between Abell and Darling-Hammond's NCTAF left any befuddled spectators willing to call the contest a draw, the U.S. Department of Education clearly was not among them. In a major report on how schools could meet the challenge in the No Child Left Behind Act of having a "highly qualified teacher" in every classroom by the end of the 2005–2006 school year, the Secretary of Education cited in an approving way Abell's debunking of the ed-schooling-is-essential research (Secretary's Annual Report, 2002). Indeed, the report also commended the work of economists Dan Goldhaber and Dominic Brewer, who found that "contrary to conventional wisdom, mathematics and science students who have teachers with emergency credentials do no worse than students whose teachers have standard teaching credentials, all else being equal" (Goldhaber and Brewer, 1999).

In fact, the whole thrust of the Education Secretary's report is to make clear that a "highly qualified teacher" as required by the new federal law will not be one and the same as a teacher "highly credentialed" by the professional schools of education. The Secretary panned the education schools as managing simultaneously to "maintain low standards and high barriers." While attracting some of the weakest students, the schools have helped erect barriers to the profession that have deterred a good many of the brightest and most motivated persons from seeking to become teachers. As will be noted in chapter 6, the game plan envisions much greater use of alternative certification to get people who know their subjects into classrooms quickly, without enduring the ed-school hoops. Nor is this, as some education establishmentarians claim, just the intent of a conservative Republican administration. No Child Left Behind was a fully bipartisan enactment, and Democratic leaders have joined in posing challenges to the existing teacher-prep monopoly.

Is the answer, then, to close down the schools of education? A fair number of critics would answer in the affirmative, but that would not necessarily be the wisest course. If schools of education operated less

like certification mills and more like providers of training to meet
market demands, they could be serving education more usefully than
they now do as a monopoly. University journalism and business schools
provide a model that could work equally well for education. No one
is forced to attend a journalism school and be certified in order to write
for or edit a newspaper; nor must an entrepreneur go to business
school and earn a state-issued piece of paper in order to work in or
start a business. But journalism and business schools prosper by offering academic programs that students decide on their own will give
them an edge in their chosen lines of work. Moreover, these schools
provide a multitude of continuing education opportunities for people
who have gone to work in business or journalism without having
majored in those fields. There is no reason schools of education could
not similarly provide training as necessary for those who have begun
teaching with arts and sciences backgrounds, or who have switched
to teaching from other careers.

But if teaching is a profession, why shouldn't the model for education be law and medicine, where there is a licensing process to guarantee competence and protect the public against fraud? A prime reason
is that law and medicine deal with closely defined bodies of knowledge that can be quantified and condensed into curricula. There is no
such canon for teaching, no consensus as to the knowledge and skills
necessary to make a good teacher, or the pedagogical approaches best
used in classrooms.

Suppose, instead of central bureaucrats adding up credits on transcripts to determine if aspiring teachers have taken enough education
courses of dubious value, local school systems allowed principals to
hire the brightest teacher candidates they could find? Suppose applicants had only to hold a college degree, pass a test of skills and knowledge relevant to the level or subject they would be teaching, and pass
a criminal background check? In a thought-provoking paper for the
centrist Progressive Policy Institute, University of Virginia professor
Frederick M. Hess suggested such simplification would spark the development of a "competitive certification" model. New teachers could
be placed under the wing of a mentor teacher and work gradually into
greater teaching responsibility. In that process, they could take in-
service training from public or private providers, including schools of
education that now would be obliged to serve individual needs instead
of enforcing a redundant sequence of courses on all license-seekers.
"In short," said Hess, "the competitive model would move teacher

certification past what is essentially a guild system and toward a meaningful professional model" (Hess, 2001).

Unlocking the gates to careers in teaching could be one important
step in the building of better teachers. But there are other steps to
be taken toward ensuring results as well as professional satisfaction,
as we shall see.

# CHAPTER 5

## *The Players*

In the contention over how to build a better American teacher, virtually all the players claim to be reformers. There may be people who want to leave undisturbed a credentialing system based largely on counting credits earned in education courses (the credit-counters in education bureaucracies, perhaps), but they are not vocal.

The self-proclaimed reformers split into two sharply opposed camps: those who believe in centralizing power over the gates to teaching careers, albeit by "professionalizing" that control, and those who advocate deregulation and decentralization of teacher preparation and licensing. So numerous are organizational components of these camps, most identified by acronyms, that a scorecard often seems a must for any outsider trying to make sense of this debate. But the most helpful way to keep the debate sorted out may be to think of the contending camps as the two powerful, but very different, baseball teams that clashed in the 2001 World Series—the New York Yankees and the Arizona Diamondbacks.

The Yankees are the proponents of the centralized model. Their team consists of many of the organizations and people long dominant in the world of teacher preparation and credentialing. The Yankees also have the backing of old money—the Carnegie and Rockefeller foundations, both headquartered in New York—as well as the federal government.

The Diamondbacks are the advocates of deregulation and a freer market for K–12 teachers. Their organizations and players tend to be newer forces in the teacher-prep game. They have foundation support from Middle America, and only with the arrival of the George W. Bush administration in Washington have they tapped the federal education budget for a little seed money. One of their leaders is even from Arizona—Lisa Graham Keegan, the former Superintendent of Public Instruction for that state who now heads the Education Leaders Council, a coalition of eight states that beg to differ with the top-down approach to education reform put forward since the 1990s.

Let's look at these two teams.

## THE YANKEES

The organizational players for this team have been on the field for many seasons. One of the most venerable is the National Council for Accreditation of Teacher Education, NCATE (pronounced *n-kate*), which is a half-century old. Since its founding by a coalition of education interests, NCATE has aspired to convince schools of education and state governments to hand over to it all authority over accreditation of teacher education. NCATE hadn't been around long before it began incurring the wrath of critics of the education establishment. "This is a relatively new organization that promises to become one of the strongest in higher education," concluded one such critic, who later added that "the most serious charge against NCATE is that it threatens to become a vast academic cartel that will ultimately prevent the employment of any person for any job at any level in any public school, and perhaps in any private school as well, who has not been through an NCATE-accredited program" (Koerner, 1963: 232).

Despite such early fears of an NCATE monolith, the organization struggled with minimal success for many years to sign up collegiate schools of education and state governments for its accrediting services. *Education Week* reported that by the late 1980s "a number of higher education officials began questioning the value of the organization and discussed the possibility of creating an alternative body" (Ponessa, 1997).

Enter the National Commission on Teaching and America's Future (NCTAF). With the backing of the Carnegie Corporation, this private panel (the membership of which reads like a Who's Who of the public education establishment) lifted NCATE out of its long slump and elevated the organization to superstar status practically overnight. By embracing a model of reform, called "professionalization," that would make NCATE the gatekeeper to all K–12 teaching jobs, NCTAF made Koerner seem prescient in warning against the rise of a cartel controlling the teaching market. Under NCTAF's recommendations, which came with its issuance of a 1996 report titled *What Matters Most: Teaching for America's Future*, no person would be allowed to teach without having been trained at an NCATE-accredited school of education. In theory, such a reform would professionalize teaching by putting the profession itself in charge of entrance standards, much as is done in the medical and legal professions. Critics charge, however, that the national teacher unions are the players with real clout, not the everyday teachers (NCTAF, 1996).

North Carolina Governor James Hunt was the founding chairman of NCTAF, and the ubiquitous Linda Darling-Hammond, education professor extraordinaire at Teachers College, Columbia University, and more recently at Stanford, was its founding Executive Director. NCTAF has remained active into the twenty-first century, continuing to lobby for its bid to shift teacher training and certification from state political authorities to private managerial agencies controlled by the "profession" itself. Its leaders showed savvy publicists' skills in generating press reports terming its report a "scathing indictment" of the status quo. They championed a "caring, competent, and qualified teacher for every child." Who could disagree with that? Packaging NCTAF as an outsider trying to tear down the education establishment's walls, however, was about as believable as it would be if the Yankees proclaimed themselves organizational renegades in the baseball world. As two noted university economists observed, "Although the NCTAF claims that its report is not the work of education insiders, the largest block of members comes from major education organizations and education schools, including presidents of the two major teacher unions, the NEA and AFT" (Ballou and Podgursky, 1997).

The second major existing entity that NCTAF anointed as a superstar was the National Board for Professional Teaching Standards (NBPTS). NBPTS and NCATE are the sultans of swat in the Yankees' lineup for centralizing power over teaching.

Like NCTAF, the NBPTS has its roots in the 1986 Carnegie Task Force on Teaching as a Profession. A national board to promulgate higher standards for the teaching profession from within was an idea favored by the late Albert Shanker, who as American Federation of Teachers president was one teacher union leader who spoke candidly when he saw sloth within the public-education system. The NBPTS got its start in 1987. Whether it is, in the early years of the new century, the kind of force for excellent teaching that Shanker envisioned is debatable. But certainly it is powerful, and growing more so by the year. It received seed money from the Carnegie Foundation and then in the 1990s, at the urging of President Bill Clinton, began to receive federal subsidies.

NCTAF wants a network of professional boards established in the 50 states to certify teachers according to NBPTS standards. At the national level, the NBPTS would certify more than 100,000 teachers, who would be presumed to be exemplars for the profession.

Thus, NCATE for teacher preparation and NBPTS for teacher certification would set the standards for all of elementary and secondary education. And NCTAF is the entity that would boost them into that catbird's seat. Yet, this would be less the result of independent actions than of a well-greased machine, or even the "interlocking directorate" that Arthur Bestor saw the education establishment resembling in the 1950s. A look at the overlapping memberships on the boards of directors of these powerful organizations (see Table 5.1) will make that clear. But consider for now how interests converge in the Yankees' clubhouse: The President of NCATE is on the board of NBPTS, and the President of NBPTS is on the board of NCATE. NCATE's founding chairman, Jim Hunt, served as chairman of NBPTS, and in addition NCATE's Executive Director, Darling-Hammond, did a stint on the NBPTS board. For certain, the footprints of the nation's largest teacher union, the NEA, are all over the lot. The President, Vice President, and Secretary/Treasurer of the NEA all serve on the NCATE board, while the NEA President and an NEA board member also serve on the NBPTS board.

This stacking of the lineups, or layering of interests, shows the Yankees have clout, but a fair question is *What good does this exercise of power do for education?* Linda Darling-Hammond's vision is of a "democratic profession of teaching" that through its own entities (such as NCATE and NBPTS) will develop high standards for learner-centered instruction based on such theorists as Harvard psychologist Howard Gardner of "multiple intelligences" fame. Such standards "share a view of teaching as complex, contingent, and reciprocal, that is, continually shaped and reshaped by students' responses to learning experiences." Darling-Hammond contrasts her vision of a teacher profession's self-generated standards with what she dismisses as an outmoded "technicist" model of teacher training based on implementing knowledge supposedly disconnected from students' real needs (Darling-Hammond, 1997). In a subsequent work written collaboratively with NCATE President Arthur Wise and RAND Corporation

Table 5.1
Partial List of Overlapping Officers, Directors, and Members

| Name of Individual | NCTAF<br>Nat'l Commission on Teaching & America's Future | NCATE<br>National Council for Accreditation of Teacher Education | NBPTS<br>National Board for Professional Teaching Standards | NEA<br>National Education Association | AFT<br>American Federation of Teachers | NAME<br>National Assoc. for Multicultural Education |
|---|---|---|---|---|---|---|
| Betty Castor | | Executive Board | President | | | |
| Robert Chase | Founding Continuing Member | Executive Board | Board of Directors | President (NFIE Board)[1] | | |
| Antonia Cortese | | Former Executive Board | Board of Directors | | Vice President | |
| Sandra Feldman | Founding Continuing Member | Executive Board | Board of Directors | | President | |
| Keith Geiger | Founding Member | | Former Board of Directors | Former President | | |
| Donna Gollnick | | Senior Vice President | | | | President |
| Linda Darling-Hammond | Exec. Director | | Former Board of Directors | (Former NFIE Board)[1] | | |
| Gov. James B. Hunt, Jr. | Chairman | | Founding Chairman | | | |
| James Kelly | Founding Member | Board Member | Founding President | | | |
| Nat LaCour | | | Founding Member | | Executive Vice President | |
| Dennis van Roekel | | Executive Board | | Sec./Treasurer | | |
| Theodore Sanders[2] | Founding Member | Former Executive Board | | (NFIE Board)[1] | | |
| Reg Weaver | | Executive Board | Former Board of Directors | Vice President | | |
| Arthur E. Wise, Jr. | Founding and Current Member | President | Board of Directors | (Former NFIE Chairman)[1] | | |

[1]NFIE (Formerly National Foundation for the Improvement of Education, now NEA Foundation for the Improvement of Education) was created by the NEA in 1969.

[2]Sanders is President of Southern Illinois University and founding President, Education Commission of the States.

Note: This chart was prepared by researchers at The Foundation Endowment in March 1998.

research scientist Stephen Klein, Darling-Hammond further expressed a conviction that in teaching, as in other professions, a consensus can be reached as to a "core of knowledge that most teachers and teacher educators would agree must be mastered by any individual who wishes to practice responsibly as a professional teacher." This "growing consensus," they concluded, also embraces a concept of teaching "based on the integration of many areas of knowledge, characterized by the use of multiple skills appropriately applied to particular situations and dependent upon considerations of students and subjects" (Darling-Hammond, Wise, and Klein, 1999: 166).

Ultimately, one has to wonder if the powerful players' fondest wishes for professionalization, however sincere they may be, are too dependent on subjective judgment to be useful in preparing teachers to help students reach high levels of academic achievement. In 2001, NCATE was touting a new set of "performance-based" standards, streamlined from the 20 it once enforced to just six. At the November annual convention of the National Association for Multicultural Education (NAME), NCATE officials explained at a private workshop (which the author of this book attended) just how the new standards would work. Perhaps NCATE was preaching to a particular choir and striking tones of multicultural advocacy more than that actually apply in normal accreditation reviews, but the chief presenter, Donna Gollnick, explained how "diversity" would be an implicit factor in education schools' implementation of four of the six standards, while a fifth standard deals explicitly with diversity. NCATE defines diversity as follows: "Differences among groups of people and individuals based on ethnicity, race, socioeconomic status, gender, exceptionalities, language, religion, sexual orientation, and geographical area." (Indicative of the close ties in recent years between NCATE and NAME is the fact that at the time Gollnick addressed the workshop she was both Senior Vice President of NCATE and President of NAME.)

The NCATE standards, adopted in 2000, pay lip service to elevating student achievement but the primary emphasis seems to lie elsewhere. Here is a summary of the standards that Gollnick dissected for the NAME workshop:

Standard 1 deals with "candidate knowledge, skills, and dispositions." Accreditation teams are supposed to ascertain if aspiring teachers "know and demonstrate the content, pedagogical, and professional knowledge, skills, and dispositions necessary to help all students learn." Accreditors look at whether various assessments show the candidates meet "professional, state, and institutional standards."

Standard 2 has to do with the assessment system and unit evaluation. NCATE teams seek to find if the education school has an assessment system to collect and analyze data regarding "applicant
qualifications, candidate and graduate performance," and how the
school operates to evaluate and to improve its programs.

Standard 3 is about field experience and clinical practice. The school
is supposed to offer aspiring teachers field experience and clinical practice so that they can "demonstrate the knowledge, skills, and dispositions necessary to help all students learn."

Standard 4 is the one that deals entirely with diversity, although
Gollnick said diversity is an integral factor in all but one of the other
five standards. Under this standard, the school is to put into practice
and evaluate "curriculum and experiences for candidates to acquire and
apply the knowledge, skills, and dispositions necessary to help all students learn." Such experiences are to include "working with diverse
higher education and school faculty, diverse candidates, and diverse
students," preschool through twelfth grade.

Standard 5 has to do with faculty qualifications, performance, and
development. In addition to being "qualified" (however that may be
defined), education-school faculty must "model best professional practices in scholarship, service, and teaching," to include assessing their
own effectiveness with the teacher candidates. The schools also are to
"systematically" evaluate faculty performance and promote professional
development.

Finally, standard 6 relates to governance and resources: The education school has the "leadership, authority, budget, personnel, facili-
ties, and resources, including information technology resources, for
the preparation of candidates to meet professional, state, and institutional standards." All of which may be doable for a large education
school within a state university, but small independent colleges oriented to the liberal arts may find such requirements hard to meet, even
though they may be graduating teachers who know academic subjects
far more thoroughly than the university ed-school products.

Although multicultural diversity is the stand-alone subject of just
one of the NCATE standards, Gollnick explained how it is embed-
ded in the other standards to be enforced in accrediting teacher-training institutions. In standard 3, dealing with field experience, for
example, NCATE will insist that this work be done "in diverse settings," even when the main campus of the school of education is
located in a rather isolated, culturally homogeneous area. With standard 5, NCATE will expect faculty to "integrate diversity in their own

teaching" in the process of modeling so-called "best practices." Even in standard 1, which mentions content "to help all students learn," accreditors are to do a "performance-based evaluation" to determine if would-be teachers exhibit what the examiners deem to be racist or sexist attitudes. A key consideration throughout is the "dispositions" of teacher candidates.

During the NCATE workshop, one of the main presenters— Professor of Education G. Pritchy Smith of the University of North Florida—made clear the thinking behind the "dispositions" criterion. Lamenting the fact that the overwhelming majority of education professors and students are white and lack "the requisite attitudes and lifestyle diversity," he suggested that NCATE and NAME advocates should be more aggressive: "We should hire people who are anti-racists and encourage them to create a new world order. Social justice is the way to close the achievement gap. This should be the central disposition."

No doubt most parents who send their children to public schools favor a good and just society, too, but what they primarily want from the schools is that their children be taught to read and write and compute (Public Agenda, 1994). The "knowledge and skills" assessed by NCATE, on the other hand, have far more to do with perpetuating progressive or learner-centered philosophy. Repeatedly the standard subtexts stress that the teacher candidates are to "facilitate" learning for all students. They are to "know how students learn and how to make ideas accessible to them." They are to "consider school, family, and community contexts in connecting concepts to students' prior experience, and applying the ideas to real-world problems."

As noted earlier, the second part of the formidable Yankees lineup is the National Board for Professional Teaching Standards (NBPTS), whose managers want it to be the powerhouse in certifying teachers in-service that NCATE is becoming in accrediting institutions that prepare future teachers. The degree of overlap between players for NBPTS and NCATE is suggestive of a well-established elite team. Like NCTAF, which sought to ensure that both parts of this Yankees team had guaranteed dominance in the field, NBPTS is an outgrowth of the 1986 Carnegie Task Force on Teaching as a Profession and a beneficiary of Carnegie largesse. Two other stalwarts in the Yankees lineup (and additions to the alphabet soup of establishment organizations) contributed guidelines for codifying what teachers need to know, consistent with the educationist worldview: the Interstate New Teacher

Assessment and Support Consortium (INTASC), a creation of the Council of Chief State School Officers, and the American Association of Colleges for Teacher Education (AACTE). The AACTE in 1989 and INTASC in 1992 produced papers on knowledge, skills, and "dispositions" (attitudes) that still inform efforts to centralize control of teacher preparation and licensing. As opposition has emerged from a team that seeks decentralization, the AACTE has lobbied to preserve the Yankees' advantage.

To be sure, the concept of a national board to advance teaching as a true profession sprang from the best of intentions. In his 1960 book, *The Future of Public Education*, Myron Lieberman, a former negotiator of teacher union contracts as well as consultant to both major teacher unions, first advocated national boards to certify teachers' excellence in specific academic disciplines (Wilcox, 1999). His idea was that such a system would assuage union leaders' fears that merit pay for teachers inevitably would be tainted by subjective judgments of school administrators. His concept lay on the table for a long time, but in 1985 he persuaded American Federation of Teachers President Albert Shanker, a union leader with an uncommon devotion to academic excellence, to take up the cause. Shanker put the idea before the Carnegie panel, and the NBPTS was on its way. Lieberman by then had grown skeptical that the board could maintain the necessary degree of independence from the unions to be a force for merit, and the subsequent composition of the 63-member board of directors tends to confirm those fears. Almost two-thirds of the directors are either members or officials of the NEA and AFT, the two major teacher unions (Wilcox, 1999). Lieberman, President of the Education Policy Institute, is today probably the nation's most knowledgeable and astute critic of the teacher unions' exercise of power to thwart reforms, such as school choice. His book, *The Teacher Unions* (1997), is a necessary read for anyone who wants to understand the arrayed powers in modern American education.

The NBPTS confers national certification on the basis of a "performance-based" process that shows a decided preference for teachers who practice that old-time progressivism of the education schools. It calls this an evaluation of "pedagogical content knowledge." Nowhere in the process is there any value-added measurement to see if a teacher has aided students in measurably raising their achievement during the school year. Instead, candidates submit portfolios of their lesson plans and their students' work and videotapes of themselves teaching in the classroom. They must pay a $2,300 application fee up front, but frequently school boards pick up the tab for them.

Thirty-three states and almost 300 school districts offer sizable bonuses (as much as $5,000 to $7,500) to teachers who successfully negotiate the NBPTS hoops, and not just one-time bonuses but yearly ones for the ten-year life of the certification (which is renewable). The NEA and AFT have displayed their eagerness that national certification spread and spread by jointly publishing a comprehensive guidebook to seeking NBPTS certification (*A Candidate's Guide*, 2001). Some of the "cameraperson" tips for teachers taping themselves are almost comically banal: Before taping, "make sure the tape is in the camera." To improve sound, avoid taping "when there is extraneous noise (e.g., band practice, recess, lawn mowing, etc. [*sic*])." Such advice suggests the NEA and AFT fret about teachers being competent enough to be just semiskilled cinematographers. More telling, however, is their repeated admonition that teacher-candidates for national certification pay attention only to the NBPTS standards, because they constitute the only criteria used to award certification. (The guidebook uses "only" in boldface three times in one sentence.) The instruction continues:

> You probably have your own standards of what you consider to be good teaching, or you may agree with another set of teaching standards. Although these teaching standards may be helpful to you in developing your teaching practice, they **should not** [boldface theirs] be your focus during the National Board Certification process. Your sole focus should be the National Board standards, because it is those—and **only** [boldface theirs] those standards—on which your work will be evaluated.

That is a remarkable piece of advice. It suggests that if teachers have developed their own philosophies based on years of proven success in elevating student learning (as teachers in chapter 2 tell of having done), they should completely ignore what works unless it happens to jibe with the practices favored by the National Board. Here we have process scoring an absolute knockout over academic results. And what might be the pedagogical approach favored by the NBPTS standards? That is not difficult to discern, simply from a perusal of the NEA/AFT guidebook to meeting the NBPTS standards. For instance, a friend of the teacher is supposed to fill out a "critical observation worksheet" to go into the applicant's portfolio after witnessing his or her teaching. This worksheet asks for evidence that the teacher has tapped the children's "natural curiosity and interests" (a dollop of Rousseau here) and has allowed for the children "to have some control of the activity" (a clear preference for progressivism over teacher-directed instruction there). Another request is for evidence that "learning experiences are designed to help children discover _____ principles for themselves." Whether "mathematical" or "scientific" or "literary" fills in the blank, that is a clear nod to the constructivist or discovery method of instruction.

Such portfolio assessment solicits subjective judgment on the nature of a teacher's work. One indicator of competence that does not interest the NBPTS is the teacher's level of literacy. By policy, the National Board deducts no points for errors in spelling, punctuation, and grammar the applicants may make in the written portion of their assessments, no matter how egregious such errors may be. Amazingly, that policy applies even to English teachers seeking the NBPTS stamp of approval. Given that most NBPTS-certified teachers are assigned as mentors for other teachers, a legitimate concern arises as to the example of verbal facility some mentors may provide for some protégés (though undoubtedly many of the nationally certified teachers are literate).

In the end, the most critical question about the National Board for Professional Teaching Standards is whether it makes a difference for the better in the American schoolhouse. A fierce dispute rages over that point. Perhaps the leading critic, the bête noire of the NBPTS—Michael Podgursky, Chairman of the Economics Department at the University of Missouri-Columbia—has persistently contended that the education establishment has undertaken "no rigorous study" to ascertain if students of NBPTS-certified teachers learn more than do students of other teachers (Podgursky, 2001). He contends that an analysis of NBPTS, funded to the tune of $500,000 by the U.S. Department of Education, precluded any legitimate test of effectiveness because it rejected out of hand taking students' standardized test scores into account. Not surprisingly, Betty Castor, the President of NBPTS, sharply disagreed. As "proof" she cited a study by researchers at the University of North Carolina-Greensboro that compared 65 teachers who had applied for the national certification, approximately half of whom received it (Bond, 2000). The team funded by the U.S. Department of Education and NBPTS found that the certified teachers did significantly better on most of the "dimensions of teaching expertise" that NBPTS assesses in its standards. But these dimensions exude a subjective quality—for instance, one assaying "multidimensional perception," defined as "demonstrating a deeper understanding of students' verbal and non-verbal responses, and using this information to prioritize instruction." Given that it was by such murky yardsticks that the NBPTS candidates were measured, it was no surprise that those winning certification did better that those who did not. That's in fact self-obvious. The still-unanswered question is *Does that make any difference in the classroom in terms of what students achieve?*

Drawing on data from the Tennessee Value-Added Assessment System for the 16 NBPTS-certified grades 3–8 teachers in Tennessee who have value-added teacher reports in the state database, Professor of Education J. E. Stone from East Tennessee State University found in May 2002 that the nationally board-certified teachers had not risen above average in bringing about increased achievement by their students (Stone, 2002). With the value-added yardstick (which is featured in chapter 8), an annual gain equaling or surpassing 115 percent of the national norm gain is regarded as "exemplary" and awarded an "A." Conversely, a gain of less than 85 percent is deemed "deficient" and given an "F." Looking at the 16 NBPTS-certified teachers collectively, Stone found that only 14 percent of scores on various subjects met the "A" standard, while 10 percent got "F"s. With the bulk of scores falling between those extremes, the achievement gains realized under NBPTS teachers were no greater than gains made under other teachers, according to Stone.

In a move typical of the fury exhibited by an education establishment scorned, the NBPTS quickly issued a release slamming Stone's work as "hardly independent research," given that the founder of the Education Consumers Clearinghouse Consultants Network had criticized the NBPTS and advocated market-based reform of teacher preparation and licensing. Of course, that ignored the reality that researchers—including those working on NBPTS's dime—rarely lack opinions about the issues they study. The relevant question is whether opinions determine the outcome. The Education Commission of the States, a pillar of the education establishment, also cast aspersions on the small study of NBPTS's effectiveness. (However, such prominent education researchers as Eric Hanushek, a senior fellow at the Hoover Institution, defended Stone's study as sound in its methodology and analysis.) The NBPTS complained that value-added data from just 16 teachers were too skimpy to permit valid conclusions, but the NBPTS itself had been touting studies of its own drawing on as few as three NBPTS-certified teachers. In any event, if the NBPTS as a Big Education producer could sponsor its own studies, why couldn't a small education consumers group do likewise without having its integrity impugned?

As 2002 began, the NBPTS did seem to be tacitly conceding the need for more substantial research establishing its effectiveness. It had put out a call for scholars to examine its processes without favor, and was marshaling donors willing to give "multiple millions of dollars" to bankroll new scholarship. It had retained a team headed by Tennessee Value-Added guru William Sanders to compare 800 teachers in North Carolina, including those who had the national certification, those who applied but didn't receive it, and those who had chosen not to apply. The results are widely anticipated, but even if they should show an achievement edge for NBPTS teachers, that would not necessarily show that the certification process brought about that good result (Archer, 2002).

Like the baseball Yankees, the education Yankees seem always to have the advantage of a bench and pockets that are both deep. But now, in the critical field of teacher preparation and licensing, they are finally getting some competition.

## THE DIAMONDBACKS

As noted in earlier chapters, critics of the education establishment's tightly controlled system of credentialing teachers have been vocal for much of the past century. Finally, on April 20, 1999, the Diamondbacks team got its game plan in order in a big way. The proponents of drawing on a much freer market to get quality teachers in the classroom issued a call to action—a manifesto—that carried considerable clout.

Released by the Thomas B. Fordham Foundation, the manifesto ran under the title *The Teachers We Need and How to Get More of Them: A Manifesto*, a slight twist on E. D. Hirsch, Jr.'s, best-selling critique of progressive education, *The Schools We Need and Why We Don't Have Them*. Indeed, Hirsch was one of the 54 original signers of the *Manifesto*. (The *Manifesto* continues to be accessible on the Internet and available to be signed at www.edexcellence.net/library/teacher.html.) Among other notable signers were the Republican governors of Michigan and Pennsylvania, John Engler and Tom Ridge; former U.S. Secretary of Education William Bennett; the Arizona Superintendent of

Public Instruction, Lisa Graham Keegan; and Pennsylvania Secretary of Education Eugene Hickok. A key player on the Diamondbacks is a veteran critic of the education establishment, Chester E. Finn, Jr., who was an Assistant Secretary of Education during the Reagan administration and who now serves as President of the Fordham Foundation. Finn's criticisms appear in many forums, especially conservative-leaning ones like the *Weekly Standard* and the *Wall Street Journal* editorial sections, and he produces a weekly online digest that he calls *The Education Gadfly*, the role he clearly relishes for himself.

The *Manifesto* depicts the regulatory strategy for elevating teacher quality as a flawed process that is likely to become even more counter-productive under proposals to make NCATE and NBPTS more powerful. The other way championed by the upstart Diamondbacks comes through in the following paragraph that follows a critique of the regulatory approach:

> A better solution to the teacher quality problem is to simplify the entry and hiring process. Get rid of most hoops and hurdles. Instead of requiring a long list of courses and degrees, test future teachers for their knowledge and skills. Allow principals to hire the teachers they need. Focus relentlessly on results, on whether students are learning. This strategy, we are confident, will produce a larger supply of able teachers and will tie judgments about their fitness and performance to success in the classroom, not to process or impression. (Kanstoroom and Finn, 1999: 2)

The *Manifesto* takes the view that there is no "one best system" for preparing and certifying teachers, though its signers clearly are fond of Teach for America, the program that puts bright liberal-arts graduates into needy classrooms without prior grounding in professional education classes. The signers believe it reasonable to pay teachers higher salaries if their fields are subjects in which teachers are in short supply, and if their teaching produces gains in student learning. They are all for giving power to principals, and letting them be held accountable for the productivity of the teachers they hire. They would not eliminate all regulations: Would-be teachers would have to pass criminal background checks, and they would have to demonstrate their subject-matter competence by majoring in that subject in college or passing a rigorous examination of their knowledge. The *Manifesto*'s authors are certain that this sort of alternative pathway to teaching will assist in getting able teachers in the nation's classrooms, although studies to prove the point are few.

From the *Manifesto* sprang the National Council on Teacher Quality (NCTQ), with largely the same cast of supporters—notably, Finn's Fordham Foundation and the Education Leaders Council. The NCTQ opened a Washington office in February 2001 and quickly became a lively presence on the Internet with a weekly E-mail bulletin, *Teacher Quality Bulletin (TQB)*, that gave blow-by-blows on the teacher-education wars. *TQB* reports from its own perspective that markets work better than regulation, of course, but does so in a highly literate and entertaining way. NCTQ's Web site has a searchable database of activity in every state on the teacher-quality front. The founding policy board featured not only Arizona's Lisa Keegan but also a former National Teacher of the Year, Tracey Bailey, who has led efforts to help independent-minded teachers form professional associations serving as alternatives to the national teacher unions. The NCTQ tapped as its President Michael Poliakoff, a former college Latin teacher who had a major hand in creating Pennsylvania's Teachers for the 21st Century initiative. In 2003, Kate Walsh, author of the Abell Foundation critique of teacher education examined at length in chapter 4, became the NCTQ's Executive Director.

Like the baseball Diamondbacks, the NCTQ progressed to the big game very quickly when in the fall of 2001 it announced plans for an American Board for Certification of Teacher Excellence (ABCTE). Support came from the education-conscious George W. Bush administration in the form of a $5 million grant from the U.S. Department of Education to help the fledgling ABCTE set up a credentialing system for both new and experienced teachers. The new Board's mission states that it "will use rigorous assessments to identify and honor teachers who demonstrate outstanding ability to impart skills and knowledge to their students and who can serve as mentors and models for other teachers." Although the ABCTE advertises itself as complementing, not supplanting, existing certification mechanisms, it clearly intends to differ sharply from the establishment's NBPTS. For instance, the ABCTE will require evidence that teachers have helped their students measurably improve their achievement, while the NBPTS does not. And while the NBPTS trains its own graders and instructs them to ignore errors in spelling, punctuation, and grammar in applicants' portfolios, the ABCTE plans to have a major testing service do the scoring according to high standards for accuracy. The ABCTE also promises that it "will ensure a robust supply of talented new teachers without relying on traditional college-of-education training." That stands in stark contrast with NCATE, which insists not only that all teachers should be products of education schools but also that they all should be products of NCATE-accredited schools of education. In a June 2003 E-mail to supporters, Keegan, Walsh, and Kathy Madigan (the experienced educator at the helm of ABCTE) offered this condensed view of their aspirations:

> American Board certification is based on rigorous standards that attest to both professional teaching and content area knowledge. Targeting recent college graduates, career-changers, and existing teachers seeking certification, [ABCTE asks candidates to] demonstrate their mastery of those areas through computer-based examinations that use multi-media technologies to replicate classroom scenarios. In addition, candidates must offer evidence of previous instructional experience and a willingness to be mentored as a beginning teacher.

That statement was in the context of what amounted to a Diamondback complaint to the Major League Baseball about foul play by the Yankees. The education Diamondbacks alleged that the education Yankees' chief Washington lobbying organization, the AACTE, had illicitly obtained and widely circulated questions that were to be used in the ABCTE's first field test. The breach of security forced the leaders of the American Board to drop the compromised questions and sever a relationship with the testing contractor that had overseen the field tests. Nevertheless, despite what they implied was a deliberate act of Yankees sabotage, they vowed to have a new set of tests ready by September 2003. Articles in the Washington press confirmed that AACTE President David Imig had distributed the ABCTE questions at an Arizona conference. However, Imig told *The Washington Post* he intended no harm because he shared the material with other professionals who understood the sensitivity of the yet-to-be-used questions (Mathews, 2003). The Chairman of the House Education Committee, Ohio Republican John Boehner, vowed to hold hearings to determine if release of the confidential information was a deliberate attempt to undermine a federally funded project.

Regardless of the final determination on Capitol Hill, this episode showed the growing intensity of competition as challengers threatened the Yankees' long domination of entry to K–12 teaching in the United States.

If another upstart organization—the Teacher Education Accreditation Council (TEAC)—has its way, institutions that train future teachers and wish to seek accreditation will have an alternative to NCATE. Incorporated in 1987, TEAC already has won the blessing of the prestigious National Council for Higher Education Accreditation, which decides which accrediting organizations are up to the task of doing intensive evaluations of collegiate academic programs. TEAC, led by Frank B. Murray, former Dean of Education at the University of Delaware in Newark, contends that NCATE's benchmarks are of unproven value and also are burdensome, especially for smaller schools. TEAC uses an auditing approach, common in the United Kingdom and elsewhere, wherein accreditors examine whether a teacher-preparation program is meeting its own goals, as well as adhering to three bedrock principles: the students have mastered content and pedagogy; the program assesses learning by a valid instrument; the school practices self-evaluation to improve continuously. TEAC, in short, is far less prescriptive than NCATE and encourages schools to think creatively. Murray likens TEAC to the editorial board of a journal. "The author writes an article and says, 'Here's the evidence,' and we evaluate it to see if it is true" (Blair, 2001). (As of mid-2002, TEAC counted more than 60 teacher-training programs as candidates, and three had won accreditation. One is the University of Virginia's Curry School, which is ranked among the top schools in the nation.)

Another emerging force for reform is the American Council of Trustees and Alumni, which is urging university trustees to examine the quality of their teacher-preparation programs and to push their presidents for change where it is needed. Its Trustees for Better Teachers project is taking a critical look at teacher education in a series of books, and in the process taking a stand for a more open, less monolithic system. Declaring the education schools' "near-monopoly" to be "highly undesirable," the Trustees' first publication asserts that, "Monopolies inhibit experimentation and discovery. There is no more reason for government to specify *the method* for training teachers than it should specify *the method* for training violinists, carpenters, or computer specialists" (Leef, 2002: iv).

Baseball analogies apply imperfectly to this or other real-life situations. But Yankees-vs.-Diamondbacks works at least to this extent: There are two teams—one long-established, the other an expansion franchise—that espouse substantially different strategies for getting high-quality teachers into K–12 classrooms. The education Diamondbacks may or may not eventually "win," but at least now there is a brisk competition of ideas. Eventually, America's children should benefit from greater intellectual diversity and depth in the teacher corps.

# CHAPTER 6

# The Roads Less Traveled

For those who believe the gates to teaching ought to be open wide, and not just to those who have taken prescribed school-of-education training, there is good news. According to C. Emily Feistritzer, who keeps closer tabs on this trend than anyone else as president of the independent, Washington-based National Center for Education Information (NCEI), 45 states offered alternative routes to teacher certification in 2002. That was up from 40 states in 2000, and a sixfold gain in states offering such nontraditional pathways since 1983, when the NCEI first began tracking this important trend. Approximately one-fourth of teachers now have degrees in fields other than education (Feistritzer and Chester, 2002).

"What we are seeing are market forces in action," Feistritzer said in a 2000 news release summarizing a trend that has continued to snowball. "People from all walks of life are stepping forward to meet the projected demand for teachers. Many of these individuals already have at least a bachelor's degree, so the old model of training teachers in undergraduate education programs does not work. States are aggressively meeting the challenge by creating new training and licensing avenues for people to enter teaching."

Cheri Yecke, who early in 2002 became the Director of Teacher Quality and Public School Choice for the U.S. Department of Education, has noted that almost one-third of newly hired teachers now are coming to classrooms without having traveled the old route through the school of education pedagogical grindstone. She calls this a "quiet revolution" that has proceeded "almost unnoticed"

(Yecke, 2002). The movement will gather much more notoriety and steam because in implementing No Child Left Behind (NCLB), the 2001 reauthorization of the Elementary and Secondary Education Act, the Department of Education is aggressively pushing to open up teaching to bright college graduates who can demonstrate they know the subjects they will be teaching, without having necessarily gone to a school of education. NCLB spells out a goal of a "highly qualified teacher" being in every classroom by the end of the 2005–2006 school year, and defines that as a bachelor's degree plus a passing score on a rigorous state examination in the subject(s) he or she will teach. This new approach does not mandate huge amounts of education courses—or, indeed, any at all—for teachers hired in the federally aided schools.

It ought to be noted that Washington's casting of a wary eye on the conventional teacher training system comes not from a Republican administration's ideological bent. In 1998 Congress passed, and President Clinton signed, a reauthorization of Title II of the Higher Education Act, which was intended to pressure states and institutions of higher education to embrace reform by reporting annually on the quality of their teacher-training programs. The schools had to report such data as the passing rates of teacher candidates on state licensing exams, and the states had to spell out their certification requirements and the numbers of teachers hired on emergency or temporary certificates. In June 2002, President Bush's Secretary of Education, Rod Paige, combined the first Title II reporting with a prospectus on how state and localities could meet the NCLB "highly qualified teachers challenge." Paige and his staff made clear that no one should cling to the old certification mill as an answer: "The Title II reporting system," he reported, "reveals that states have a long way to go in meeting these requirements, largely because of states' outdated certification systems. Many academically accomplished college graduates and mid-career professionals with strong subject matter backgrounds are often dissuaded from entering teaching because the entry requirements are so rigid. At the same time, too many individuals earn certification even though their own content knowledge is weak. States' systems seem to maintain low standards and high barriers at the same time" (Secretary's Report, 2002). Many teacher-training administrators practice deception to conceal their failure rates (for instance, by reporting pass/fail rates only *after* would-be teachers had been accepted into their programs).

However, the reporting system did produce the revealing finding that among the 29 states using the popular Praxis skills test for teacher licensure, only one state (Virginia) set its passing scores at or above the national average in reading, writing, and math. Fifteen states were so shameless as to set their passing scores below the 25th percentile. The overall passing rates exceeded 90 percent, but with the bar so low, those scores were virtually meaningless. The Praxis I test itself is not exactly the stuff of rocket science. One sample question asks would-be teachers which of the following is equal to a quarter of a million: (1) 40,000 (b) 250,000 (c) 2,500,000 (d) 1/4,000,000 (e) 4/1,000,000. Another asks for insertion of the correct choice in this sentence: Martin Luther King, Jr. [insert the correct choice] for the poor of all races: (a) spoke out passionately (b) spoke out passionate (c) did spoke out passionately (d) has spoke out passionately (e) had spoken out passionate (Clowes, 2001).

Despite evidence of the mixed quality of their product, many education deans were seeking to spin the NCLB "highly qualified teacher" mandate as one that would lower standards as states desperately seeking to fill their faculties hired uncertified teachers on emergency waivers, using dumbed-down qualification tests. But California Congressman George Miller, the ranking Democrat on the House Education Committee and a key player in negotiating a bipartisan NCLB, wasn't buying that. Rushing to hire incompetent teachers would be a "mindless response," said Miller, who noted that results of required tests of student knowledge, such as the National Assessment of Educational Progress, would tell the tale on any state that lowered teacher standards.

"We used the term 'highly qualified,'" said Miller "because we're not convinced the term 'certified' implies . . . competency" (Blair, 2002). Thus, key writers of federal law and regulation on aid to education—Democrat and Republican alike—appear to be united in the belief that there should be many routes to teaching, so long as there is a way to ensure that teachers know their stuff and are effective. As Congress prepared for the 2003 reauthorization of Title II, that consensus appeared to be holding. The House Education Committee approved without dissent a bill that would close reporting loopholes for education schools as well as provide states numerous incentives to create routes to teaching licensure that do not require amassing of education credits.

The NCEI's 2002 report yielded additional data about teachers entering classrooms via nonconventional routes that provided hope for the future if these pathways indeed do grow broader with further nudges from Washington. For instance, these teachers are more likely to teach where the demand is greatest, such as inner cities and remote rural areas, and they are more likely to help fill the need for teachers in mathematics, science, and special education (which is a positive, assuming they have subject-matter mastery to teach in those areas). Additionally, they are older than the average teacher (which sometimes translates to more mature) and more likely to be males and members of minority groups. They also are more likely to remain in teaching than those who come through schools of education (Feistritzer and Chester, 2002).

Of course some of the states offer truer, freer alternative pathways than do others. Some allow entrance to the classroom on emergency licenses but require the new teachers quickly to take a heavy load of education course work. For instance, a perusal of the NCEI's 432-page guide to such programs shows that one of New York's alternative teacher certification transitional programs will allow a liberal arts graduate with a 3.0 cumulative grade-point average to begin as a mentored teacher—but *only* after completion of 200 clock hours of pedagogical study. And after that "introductory component," the alternate-route teacher must continue with "part-time collegiate study in pedagogy, while teaching" in order to qualify for a provisional or initial certificate. Such requirements look like the mindless barriers that Secretary Paige and Capitol Hill have identified and challenged.

Teachers interviewed for this book differed greatly, partly depending on their own experiences, as to the desirability of letting people teach who had not been through an approved regimen of how-to-teach courses. There was a strong strain of thinking to the effect that "Well, I had to take all these courses and jump through all these hoops and pay all that tuition, so why should others be able just to breeze in and fill a teaching job?" A fourth-grade teacher in South Carolina observed that teachers had "earned the right" to teach by taking all the required courses. "It would be hard for someone to come in and teach without basically 'paying the price' to do it," she said. "But," she conceded, "yes, it could be done." In San Jose, California, another teacher said alternative certification is a tough question for her because she is passionate about teaching and hates to see bad teachers in the classroom. She would grudgingly allow career-switchers if they have relevant experience and go through a boot-camp-type basic training to get at least a rudimentary grasp of assessment, stages of learning, lesson plans, and the like. But if these newcomers decide they want to stay, they should have to take the full credentialing program, she believes. A pre-K teacher hailing from Montana was more blunt: "All teachers should be required to take education classes. . . . If you want to be a teacher, then take the classes." And a first-grade teacher in Rhode Island wondered, "If teachers are continually receiving professional development, how can someone without any background become an effective teacher?"

In contrast, Peggy Downs, a third-grade teacher who is also among the founding families of a charter school in Colorado, believes that people from outside professional education bring "many gifts and perspectives [that] will enrich our classrooms, especially in the middle and high school levels. The craft of teaching can be learned by those who have a natural talent. The years of expertise in a subject area are more difficult to come by. We should not hinder their contributions with an overload of educational theories and vague (sometimes questionable) philosophies. A well-supervised training period within a school that has clearly defined expectations and curriculum should be sufficient to allow them to successfully teach in the classroom."

Audrey Marie Pruitt, a third-grade teacher in northern California, said, "There are people out there who would make wonderful teachers. They are the naturals of our profession. But putting them into a classroom unsupervised is a horrible mistake. If they are very closely monitored and have a great support system, it is a feasible thing to do." But, she added, "I hope they wouldn't be paid as much as those of us who have spent years in school to get that degree and credential."

Daniel S. Konieczko, a middle/high school science teacher from Maine, preferred to put the emphasis on results:

Well-educated and subject-knowledgeable people should be brought into the classroom with minimal education courses but with solid mentoring. Knowledge begets knowledge. The public school system is designed, through its certification process and reliance on ticket-punching education courses, to keep too many qualified people out of the classroom. This is a focus on inputs as opposed to outputs. Teaching is a skill, but it is about passing on a defined and articulated body of knowledge and skills.

> Put a teacher in the classroom, tell that teacher the expected standards, and test the students on a regular basis. Either the teacher is teaching or is not. Keep the ones who produce and wash out the ones who are not producing. Teaching emphasis should be on what the students are learning and not what the teachers profess to know.

Not surprisingly, some who have come to teaching by non-conventional routes were most strongly in favor of alternative certification. Their resumes also tend to support the idea that K–12 classes would be more interesting and insightful, especially at the middle and high school levels, with the welcome mat extended to persons such as these. Consider John Tuepker, whose well-developed teaching philosophy we discussed in chapter 2. He came to teaching in Long Beach, Mississippi, via an alternate route, after two years as a Peace Corps volunteer in Sierra Leone (West Africa) and 20 years as a self-employed businessman engaged in farming, farm equipment manufacturing, and construction. Surely someone who has gained such "real world" experience would have much to share in lectures or conversations with students.

Tuepker also came to teaching with a master's degree in history, which he considers "extremely helpful in creating interesting and valuable lessons for my history students," as opposed to education courses, for which he sees "no value." To be certified, he had to have a bachelor's degree and a passing score on the minimal teaching entrance tests—plus 12 hours of education courses. One requirement was for a three-hour course in education research, but Tuepker fought that, given that he had completed a more rigorous Methods of History Research course only recently. It took him two years, but bureaucratic gatekeepers finally gave him full certification without the ed-research course.

"I am a strong supporter of recruiting people from outside education, at least at the middle school and high school level," said Tuepker. "There should be some rigorous tests and a mandated mentoring period. Pedagogical studies *detract* from the professionalism of the accomplished high school teacher."

Another teacher who brought a rich variety of experience to the classroom in lieu of a standard education degree is Dennis M. Rafferty, who in January 2001 was beginning his fourth semester at Pahoa High School on the Big Island of Hawaii, teaching special education classes to at-risk students in grades 9–12. This is how Rafferty described his preteaching experiences:

I was a young athlete. I went to Vietnam and came home as a staff sergeant. I moved on, to Alaska, where I became a fishing captain for ten years after learning the craft for almost that many years. I took my crew westward past the Islands of the Four Mountains and on to Attu each year, pursuing halibut, black cod, and any other form of ocean life that could make us a dollar. I became a union journeyman carpenter during these days to help work on projects in my community of Petersburg, Alaska. I helped build the oil dock, the new harbor, and numerous buildings, including the headquarters for the U.S. Forest Service. I came to Hawaii to build a $20 million complex on the beach at Lanikai, on the island of Oahu, for the hair-care magnate Paul Mitchell, when he was still with us.

Rafferty engaged in other exciting development projects before being hired by the National Park Service as a carpenter for work within the Volcanoes Park, where he now lives. He was attracted to teaching by a desire to make a difference in the lives of children affected by the progression of colonial settlement, and found that the Hawaii Department of Education would give him a temporary certificate, contingent upon his completing professional courses they specify. To his bachelor's degree in communications he now has added 27 units in education at the undergraduate and graduate levels. But that is not enough to satisfy the education bureaucracy that his temporary credential should become permanent.

"To cut to the quick," said Rafferty, "they want another twenty grand out of me before they'll grant tenure. I find the scholarship practiced by each of these programs to be shoddy, antiquated, and nonproductive. Endless variations on B. F. Skinner's behavioral modification theory are taught by a parade of D.O.E. [Department of Education] hacks who have a limited understanding of philosophy and psychology." Rafferty contends that Hawaii's certification is more about gatekeeping than advancing quality, and that "teachers who lack the ability to connect with children are certified over teachers who refuse to succumb to the bureaucratic demands."

*Honolulu Advertiser* columnist Cliff Slater provided independent support for Rafferty's charges when he checked into why more than half of the state finalists for the 2001 Presidential Awards for Excellence in Mathematics and Science Teaching were teachers in private schools, despite the fact private schools enroll only 16 percent of Hawaii's children. Slater discovered an answer in the person of one of the finalists—Joan Rohrback, who has a doctorate in science, plus

15 years of teaching experience. Despite those stellar credentials, Rohrback cannot win certification to teach in the public schools. Why? She has not taken the requisite school-of-education courses. Slater found another case study in state legislator Guy Ontai, who is similarly deemed unqualified to teach in Hawaii's government-run schools even though he has a master's degree in physics from the Massachusetts Institute of Technology and has been an assistant professor at West Point.

Slater's comment: "Common sense tells us that school principals worth their salt would grab these teachers. But they cannot—there are DOE rules. . . . The rules, however idiotic, do have a purpose. They provide protection for the power structure. Our insecure DOE bureaucrats must constantly attempt to show that they and their central controls cannot be replaced" (Slater, 2002).

Judging from comments on both sides of this issue, sparks could fly in faculty meetings where traditionally certified and unconventionally certified noneducation majors expressed their beliefs about the superiority of one approach or the other. Don Crawford, the teacher-contrarian who took issue with the choosing of "best teachers" in chapter 2, makes a salient point about the potential downside of alternate certification (though he supports it): "In the current system, the culture in the schools works to maintain the status quo; therefore, the fresh ideas of teachers from outside will be squashed if they go into the typical schools. You quickly learn that you can't flunk students who don't have the necessary skills, you can't kick out the students who don't display the necessary cooperativeness, and you can't give really low grades to the students who don't make an effort. A private school with a strong discipline policy . . . could easily mentor someone into their own school's philosophy and methods, and that individual could become an excellent teacher. Or a school with a strong tradition of Direct Instruction could mentor someone into that school's philosophy and methods. But most public schools would mentor a teacher into mediocrity and baby-sitting, despite their best attitude." (The pros and cons of mentoring will be the subject of chapter 7.)

Teach for America (TFA) is not an alternate route to certification, but it is a program with a track record tending to show the value of broadening the intellectual mix of the teaching corps. A remarkable young woman named Wendy Kopp began TFA when she was still a student at Princeton University in the late 1980s. Her vision was that the privileged, well-educated members of the "Me Generation" ought to have the opportunity to give something back to the country by committing to teach at least two years in the neediest inner-city and rural public schools. Since 1990, more than 5,000 members of the TFA corps have taught in schools from South Central LA to Southeast D.C., and plenty of hardscrabble places in between, like the Mississippi Delta. The numbers are not huge, but TFA and its alumni not only have made a difference in many children's lives but also have become a factor in the debate over the future face of K–12 teaching.

Primarily the TFA recruits have excelled in the liberal arts at their universities; they have not had school-of-education training. That is an affront to the Yankees, the pro-regulatory team identified in chapter 5, and a ray of hope for the Diamondbacks.

In 1994, when the program was barely out of its infancy, Yankees superstar Linda Darling-Hammond already was excoriating TFA in an article in the prestigious education-establishment organ *Phi Delta Kappan*. In her recent book, Wendy Kopp recalled that the article felt "like a punch in the chest" and seemed to be more of a personal attack than a serious academic analysis (Kopp, 2001). According to Kopp, Darling-Hammond's "evidence" consisted of inferences she drew from one *Newsday* article. For instance, Darling-Hammond wrote that "of several recruits the article covered, a number of them were in 'extreme doubt' and three quit before the first week of school was over, leaving their students with no teachers at all and their schools scrambling to find substitutes." In fact, Kopp stated, the *Newsday* article, which followed one TFA member for his first week of school in September 1990, when the program was just starting, reported that only three of the 177 corps members who had been placed in New York had not completed their first week. It further quoted the principal of the school where this TFA corps member and five others were assigned as expressing delight with their enthusiasm and commitment. The principal marveled that she practically had to chase them away at the end of the day—"they won't leave." Kopp wrote a restrained letter to the *Kappan*, seeking to correct what she thought were the most serious distortions, only to find that "Darling-Hammond replied with a harsh letter of her own, four times as long as mine, which was printed in the same issue."

It is instructive that the dominant gatekeepers to teaching seem to view the smallest deviations from orthodox monopoly control to be a threat. Remember that in chapter 4, Darling-Hammond delivered a reply to the Abell Foundation's critique of teacher certification that was longer than the critique itself. Again, this episode confirms the perceptiveness of Arthur Bestor in the 1950s in commenting on the education establishment's allergic reaction to all dissent and proposals for reform.

Of course, the other side, the Diamondbacks, likes to trumpet TFA as evidence that extensive ed-school training is not essential for successful learning by K–12 children. The issue came to a boil in August 2001 with the release of an evaluation of TFA's impact in the Houston schools that had been sponsored by that key Diamondbacks' entity, the Fordham Foundation. The respected Center for Research on Education Outcomes (CREDO) at Stanford University conducted the study with Fordham's support. CREDO found that TFA teachers performed "as well as, and in many cases better than other teachers hired by HISD [Houston Independent School District]." In a foreword, Fordham's Chester Finn and Marci Kanstoroom touted the study as a rebuke to Darling-Hammond's contention that the TFA perpetuates inequality by spreading the notion that uncertified teachers (whom Darling-Hammond considers, ipso facto, unqualified) can teach poor and minority children just as effectively as fully certified teachers. Predictably, that elicited another blast of outrage from Darling-Hammond's National Commission on Teaching and America's Future. And so the contest rages, more spirited even than the real Yankees/Diamondbacks Series.

There remain, though, the data suggesting that TFA recruits tend to do rather well in their two years of service. In response to the NCTAF, CREDO was a bit more modest than Fordham had been in stating what had been learned: "Unlike the commission, we do not claim to have the singular right answer to the problem of teacher supply and teacher performance. A great deal more analysis of the type found in the Teach for America study is needed before we can generalize about the various options and their worth. Until then, we think it better to maintain an open mind about what works best for America's schools" (Raymond, 2001).

A national program that (unlike TFA) does lay out an alternate route to certification—Troops to Teachers (TTT)—has drawn little heat from the education establishment, no doubt because it does have its recruits take education courses to become state-certified. Nevertheless, TTT has furnished fresh blood for K–12 teaching by supporting retired military personnel who wish to make the transition to teaching. The program began in 1993 as part of Department of Defense downsizing. Currently, persons separating from the military services after at least six years can receive a $5,000 stipend to help pay for completing a teacher certification program. If they agree to teach in a "high needs" district where at least half of pupils come from low-income families, their stipend can rise to $10,000. Troops must commit to teach at least three years. Both President Bush and First Lady Laura Bush have strongly endorsed this program as a way to diversify the teaching force with mature and experienced individuals, and funding is on the rise. Visibility is, too. It certainly doesn't hurt that the 2002 National Teacher of the Year—Chauncey Veatch, a social studies teacher at Coachella Valley High School in California—is a TTT product.

Several states have launched their own programs to smooth the paths of career-switchers into the classroom. Teach for Georgia is one example. Under the leadership of the reform-minded Democratic Governor Roy Barnes, the state instituted this fast-track preparation program in the summer of 2001 as a way to address the teacher shortage. The heart of the program is intense summer institutes to train career-switchers in the how-to basics of teaching, with that initial introduction to be followed by two years of close supervision on the job. The *Atlanta Journal-Constitution* reported on July 4, 2001, that "thousands of people have answered the state's call for business professionals to give up their careers and become teachers." Many were leaving higher-paying positions in order to have a chance to make a difference in children's lives. Who says idealism is dead? The popularity of this approach exceeded official expectations. Instead of the expected 100, the state filled more than 700 Teach for Georgia slots and had to turn hundreds more away (Donsky, 2001).

Typically, "fast-track" or alternative certification entails hiring college graduates and over the summer giving them a crash course in classroom mechanics to which education schools devote years. Georgia's new Business to Teaching program, for instance, has the new recruits start teaching right away while completing their education course work one night a week and in the summer. New York City's Teacher Opportunity Program lays out a seven-week course in the nitty-gritty of classroom management for math and science specialists willing to teach in the Big Apple's schools.

Universities are joining school districts and states in organizing alternative preparatory programs to put more teachers into K–12 classrooms. In January 2000, *The Chronicle of Higher Education* reported that approximately 250 institutions of higher learning now offer these "alternate routes" to teaching for persons whose jobs or college degrees have been in fields other than education. Most have started since 1990. A notable example, which harkens also to the TTT model, is the Military Career Transition Program at Old Dominion University (ODU), which is located near the naval base in Norfolk, Virginia. ODU has assisted more than 1,250 officers and senior enlisted personnel in preparing to become schoolteachers in 47 states (Basinger, 2000).

New programs claiming to ease the way into teaching for career-switchers and arts-and-sciences graduates seemingly spring up almost every day in the United States. Some truly make the break with orthodoxy and draw on the employment market, while others have not cut the umbilical cord to the schools of pedagogy. Whether embracing real reform or not, however, these new programs almost surely will be reported by the online Teacher Quality Clearinghouse (found at www.nctq.org), a service of the National Council on Teacher Quality (one of the Diamondbacks). The Clearinghouse reports not only on alternative certification but also on unconventional recruiting, reform of teacher education, subject-matter knowledge, pedagogy, teacher tests, and other timely issues of teacher preparation and certification. It is becoming an indispensable source of information. In the spring of 2002, one could read of such developments as Florida's legislature considering a bill that would free schools of state rules preventing them from hiring uncertified candidates as principals; a North Carolina judge ruling that the state has a responsibility to see to it that there are quality teachers for all students; the University of Southern Maine opening an alternative route for aspiring teachers but still requiring them to take pedagogical classes at night after their full days of teaching; and First Lady Laura Bush and former First Lady and current U.S. Senator from New York Hillary Rodham Clinton joining in an appeal to midcareer professionals considering career change to give serious thought to teaching.

Alternative certification that bypasses the entrenched monopoly will continue to be controversial, and indeed unpopular with the entrenched monopolists—many of the education-school deans and professors, state education bureaucracies, and the national associations with a vested interest in keeping the closed system shut tight. However, with everyone from the First Lady to civic leaders, and university presidents and congressmen on both sides of the aisle, and school-choice activists working hard to demolish senseless barriers to teaching, it is likely that alternative certification's greatest growth is still to come.

CHAPTER 7

# *Mentors, Mentors, Who's Got the Mentors?*

Falls Church High School, nestled in the northern Virginia suburbs of Washington, D.C., seemingly has a mentor for every type of beginning teacher, whether the teacher has been through a traditional preparatory path or not. Consider just three who have been taken under the wing of Sandy Gutiérrez in the school's Languages Department and then matched with mentors.

First, there's first-year teacher Will Carter, who, as a senior at Syracuse University with a major in communications (TV, radio, film) and Spanish, had no real idea what he wanted to do with his life. Then Carter heard that an assistant was needed in a summer program for English as a Second Language (ESL) students at a high school in Reston, near his home in northern Virginia. He did the summer stint and became hooked on teaching. But making the jump to a full-time teaching job in the fall still looked like something only a stuntman would want to attempt.

The influence of an experienced mentor helped Carter settle in quickly at Falls Church High. It really helps, he said, "to have someone in your department you can talk to." Carter was assigned to teach ESL Level 3 students—the highest level before moving on to English 9—and his mentor had taught the same class. That was fortuitous, because the class is taught without a textbook, and Carter needed all the help he could get in mustering teaching resources.

In contrast to Carter, Hope Bolfek had decided way back in high school that she wanted to be a teacher. She explored teaching as a career in a special program cosponsored by the University of Virginia and *Readers Digest*, and then went to Virginia Tech to continue her studies. There she started as an English major, then double-majored in English and Spanish, and finally earned her master's degree in curriculum and instruction. Along the way, she enjoyed an internship that allowed her to spend two days a week in a high school, assisting a teacher and even being allowed to do some teaching throughout the schoolday.

So Bolfek took her first full-time teaching job with a lot of experience already logged. The first two years of teaching she wasn't assigned a mentor, but when she arrived at Falls Church High School for year three, she was—and she's glad. "I don't think I would have attended all the conferences if I hadn't had a mentor to encourage me," she said. "This county [Fairfax] is so big, teachers don't know what is available"—for instance, a large media center that can help teachers who seek it out with using the many forms of technology to bolster their teaching.

Another benefit of the mentor/protégé relationship is that young teachers receive the benefit of being able to observe more experienced teachers in the classroom and to learn from their classroom management styles. Learning about classroom management is among the most valuable experiences of mentoring, said the third Falls Church teacher, Ellen Reilly, who came to teaching after having been a sign language interpreter in Fairfax programs during the evening. She knew the county and something of the school system, but found that having a mentor was helpful.

The attrition rate among beginning teachers is among the most acute problems in American education. Close to 40 percent of teachers leave the field within the first five years of teaching; hence, the right kind of mentoring could help stabilize teacher supply and demand. It is important, says Sandy Gutiérrez, who has been a leader in advancing mentoring at Falls Church through both a schoolwide program and a smaller, specially funded one, that the mentor be a "nurturing" person, as opposed to a "know-it-all person."

By no means do all public schools in Virginia or other states have this kind of well-developed mentoring system. One state that has placed mentors near the center of broad-based reform of teacher preparation and certification is New Jersey. In 1984, the Garden State initiated the Provisional Teacher Program, which amounted to the nation's first alternative teacher certification program (Klagholz, 2000). Although many states now claim to be offering alternate routes to the classroom, none has as comprehensive an approach as New

Jersey's, which still offers states serious about reform of teacher licensing the most sagacious model available.

The prime architect of this plan is a lifelong educator, Leo Klagholz, who devised the Provisional Teacher Program while serving as Director of Teacher Preparation and Certification in the State Department of Education in the reform-minded administration of Governor Tom Kean. Klagholz later served as Commissioner of Education for Governor Christie Whitman. The description that follows comes from Klagholz's *Growing Better Teachers in the Garden State*, an impressive account he penned for the Thomas B. Fordham Foundation in January 2000, and from my own supplementary interviews and E-mail discussions with him.

New Jersey embarked upon a dual path of reform: (1) elevate the quality of formal teacher preparation in the colleges; (2) create the "alternate route" into the profession of teaching for those who chose not to study education in college. What perhaps made the difference is that the principles applied to both pathways to teaching were similar. For teachers coming from both directions, the ideal preparation would blend a well-rounded liberal arts education with practice teaching under the eye of an experienced mentor. Unlike some other states, New Jersey addressed the totality of the problem, and, while critical of many education courses, did not simply engage in the popular sport of education-school bashing. Like many of the thoughtful teachers quoted in chapter 2, New Jersey's reformers saw a place for revamped schools of education focused on the actual needs of school districts rather than arcane theory. "A natural evolution occurred," said Leo Klagholz, in recalling why New Jersey succeeded where so many other states have failed. "Momentum just built for change and reform."

The groundwork began to be laid in 1978 with the legislatively created Commission to Study Teacher Preparation in New Jersey Colleges (CSTPP), which was composed of lawmakers, educators, and private citizens. The CSTPP found that the state's certification mandates were resulting in education courses constituting as many as 80 credits out of the 120 credits required for a teaching degree. Furthermore, it found that many of these ubiquitous courses lacked rigor or substance new teachers could put to use. Not only were future teachers majoring in education, but many of them were using education-related courses such as "Teaching Math in Elementary School" to satisfy their meager liberal arts requirements. While other college students took more rigorous mathematic courses, those who would teach math took watered-down courses about the processes of teaching math. The CSTPP also brought to light the sad reality that education courses were tending to attract the weakest students in the universities. Prospective education majors from the state's high schools were ranking 22 among 23 college majors in SAT scores, a sad situation not uncommon in other states.

The State Board of Higher Education seized upon and refined the CSTPP's recommendations via yet another blue-ribbon panel, and agreed that henceforth all aspiring teachers would have to have a liberal arts or sciences major. They could have a major in education only if it was the "secondary emphasis in a dual major." And the second big change was that all college students preparing to be teachers would be placed under the tutelage of an experienced teacher, beginning with a brief introduction in the sophomore year and culminating with a full semester of practice teaching in the senior year.

Given the adoption of those two guiding principles—a liberal arts background and mentor-assisted training in the classroom—it was not a large leap, Klagholz recalls, to construct an "alternate route" for other liberally educated persons who did not specifically prepare to be teachers in college. School districts would be freed to hire liberal arts graduates and match them with mentor teachers. These teachers coming from an unconventional route would be honing their skills in essentially the same way as the products of the reformed, traditional, via ed-school route.

Remember the hints of resentment among conventionally certified teachers quoted in chapter 6? They didn't say it quite this bluntly, but they seemed to be driving at this point: "Sure, I hated many of those education courses I had to take in college. I found them largely irrelevant to the challenges I actually faced in the classroom. But by golly, if I had to take them, then where do these alternatively certified teachers get off getting the same job with the same pay scale as I without having to take those courses? They should have to suffer as I had to." Well, Leo Klagholz points out that one of the beauties of having parallel tracks to teaching is that such resentment is largely quelled. All teachers come from liberal arts backgrounds and have done practice teaching under a mentor, regardless of whether they set out to be teachers when they were 18- or 19-year-old college students.

The groundbreaking "alternate route" reform would go through several more stages of refinement and political compromise in New Jersey before final adoption. One particularly useful exercise was a

Department of Education study to determine which education courses ought to be jettisoned and which ought to be preserved in the reformed "traditional" route to certification. The study found that a great many of the education courses which had been required, bearing such titles as "Discovering Your Teaching Self," were highly dispensable and in fact should disappear as mandates. However, at the same time, the study did not go so far as to say all professional education study is useless. It affirmed the existence of core "how-to-teach" or applied knowledge to which every new teacher should be exposed, but it emphasized that letting such exposure occur during the first year of teaching should be entirely acceptable.

Schools of education still have a role to play—"but not 80 credits out of 120," Klagholz commented. The New Jersey way was also revolutionary in making such schools the servants, not the masters, of school districts. Instead of schools and districts being subject to course-counting mandates hatched in these schools (and among their graduates in the education bureaucracy), the education schools' training programs were to be responsive to the districts' hiring needs. That is what the eggheads like to call a "paradigm shift"—and a profound and useful one indeed.

Statistical tables in Klagholz's impressive study for the Fordham Foundation (available at www.edexcellence.net) show how the "alternate route" has performed as an integral part of New Jersey's reformed system of preparing and certifying teachers. In brief:

- By the 1998–1999 school year, 457 school districts had used the program to hire teachers.
- Applicants who came via this less-traveled path attained higher scores on licensing tests than did teachers prepared in the traditional (though reformed) manner.
- Attrition rates for those coming via the alternate route were lower than rates for the traditionally prepared. During the five-year pilot period, the first-year attrition rate for provisional teachers was 6.4 percent, versus 18 percent for traditionally prepared teachers.
- Significantly, the alternate route/Provisional Teacher Program became the "dominant source of minority teachers for both urban and suburban schools." While minority enrollment in traditional teacher-prep programs had remained consistently below 10 percent, minority-group members constituted 28 percent of the provisional teachers hired by public schools. Although many higher-paying careers beckon minorities and lead diminishing numbers to major in education, it appears that some change their

minds and decide that teaching would be a more fulfilling pursuit. A program like New Jersey's makes it easier for bright young people not to be locked into early career choices.

New Jersey's proven reform contrasts with the theoretical reform offered by the National Commission on Teaching and America's Future, the mainstay of the Yankees' lineup in chapter 5. The Commission asserts that a teacher of quality is one who majored in college in the subject to be taught and who also has "intensive preparation in teaching." The first part of that construction is beyond much dispute. An aspiring teacher should have a subject-matter major. But what is meant by "intensive" how-to-teach preparation? The Commission evidently deems multiple credits in pedagogical courses a necessity because it defines a low-quality teacher, in part, as one who has taken "only a handful of education courses." Yet the New Jersey experience shows that a better way exists than just counting education credits. Hiring teachers who know their subjects and letting them learn classroom procedures under the practiced eye of a mentor or master teacher is a system that works.

Furthermore, this is exactly what private schools, as well as colleges and universities, do. No one argues that *their* teachers are inferior because they were not steeped in mandatory theory of education courses when they were undergraduates. Why should it be any different for elementary and secondary teachers?

When mentors occupy an important role in acclimating new teachers to teaching, how they are selected and placed becomes an important consideration. There seems to be wide agreement that setting up an Office of Mentoring in the central education bureaucracy is not the best way to go. Klagholz said New Jersey purposely decided to leave implementation of mentoring at the district level. Our teacher from Maine (quoted in chapter 2), Daniel Konieczko, points out that "the drawbacks to mentoring tend to become manifest when mentoring is a forced fit and is done because it has to be done as opposed to being done because it will benefit the teacher." He believes principals should do the mentor selecting in collaboration with the teachers who are to be mentored and the teachers who will be the mentors.

It is important, first and foremost, that a good personnel fit be made. Teachers who find that their mentors know less about subject materials and teaching than the teachers being mentored will not respond positively and the exercise will be futile. A drawback to mentoring can occur when the mentoring is used to develop the style of the teacher being mentored.

Critics say this puts too much emphasis on the mentor. True enough, mentoring can become just another buzzword without meaning if teachers are merely assigned a mentor for the sake of having a mentor, and there's little follow-up or rapport (Wong, 2001: 46, 50). However, the school's principal is the key figure. Given the authority in the first instance to hire the most capable teaching candidates, regardless of their education pedigrees, the principal then has the motivation to see to it that these new hires have veteran teachers to take them under their wing. Call them mentors or master teachers or just helpful colleagues—they can help the school community acclimate the new teachers to schoolday routine and prepare them for such challenges as dealing with unruly students.

As far as criticisms of the use of mentors for those who come to teaching by an alternate route, Klagholz notes that traditional college preparatory plans use exactly the same approach. That is, they place undergraduates in public schools where they "learn by doing" with the guidance of an experienced teacher assigned them by the principal. Thus, the use of experienced mentors is a strategy shared by traditional and alternate programs. And generally they rely on the same persons.

While unevenness of effort is common to all massive undertakings, "the concept of actually teaching under supervision of an experienced person is time-tested and generally considered the most valuable aspect of teacher induction. Pursuit of the ideal is a continuing—perhaps never-ending—task."

As for the principal, he or she is the proper person to be in charge, because the principal is the one person licensed by the state to evaluate teachers and supervise their development. The principal, therefore, is a natural focus of efforts to improve teaching. Unfortunately, Klagholz added, "state certification has been a crutch that has encouraged overreliance and lack of initiative by principals. Pulling away artificial crutches, then, has to be part of the process."

One caveat concerns organizations' possible use of mentors to promote noneducational agendas. The National Education Association, through its Foundation for the Improvement of Education, has published an extensive guide to creating mentoring programs in which virtually all of the "experts" quoted are officials of local teacher unions (www.nfie.org/publications/mentoring.htm). One state union official advocates that the conditions of mentoring be stipulated in collective bargaining agreements between union and school district, which would make mentoring a product of an adversarial rather than a collegial process. Another cautions against providing extra pay or stipends for mentors, because that might create "envy" that would be the "ruin-ation" of the program. That caution appears to be in accord with NEA doctrine that teacher pay be on lockstep scales, with no differentia-tion for extra performance, whether guiding fellow teachers or help-ing students make outstanding academic progress. At another point, an NEA official stresses that mentors should not substitute for "rig-orous, university-based preservice teacher preparation programs." Translated, the NEA (as indicated by its strong backing of NCATE, noted in chapter 5) wishes to make mentoring a tool of the status quo, not of reform.

By no means is mentoring the magical tool for building a better teacher. But under the direction of a strong principal, the single most important leader in education, mentoring can be part of a kit for making teacher preparation and certification more inviting to a con-genial mix of bright people who want to teach children.

# CHAPTER 8

# *Value-Added Teaching*

High-stakes testing of students has become the sharpest arrow in the quiver of would-be reformers of public elementary and secondary education—and not without justification. No matter how high standards are set for English and math and history and science, education requires some form of measurement to confirm that students are mastering the material. Unless there are consequences for failure on these tests, students and school staffs will not take them seriously. As former Virginia Superintendent of Public Instruction Bill Bosher has said, "Without testing, standards are mere suggestions."

Moreover, as public opinion surveys have repeatedly shown, parents by substantial margins support standardized testing. A survey done for the Committee for Economic Development found that about three-fourths of respondents thought the quantity of student testing in their communities was either about right or not enough (CED, 2000). Parents believe testing yields valuable information. They want to be able to compare their children and their schools against other children and their schools. Information is power. Tests provide information to consumers, and results will be critical as education begins to operate more like a free market. Objective testing is like an annual doctor's checkup or an audit by an external auditor.

Tests also serve as a valuable confirming device for grading systems that vary from school to school and teacher to teacher. Bill Evers, a research fellow at the Hoover Institution and member of Hoover's Koret Task Force on K–12 Education, observes that a pupil's grade is based not merely on achievement and exertion but also on what the teacher expects from students in his or her class. One teacher may have lower expectations for students than another teacher. One teacher may want to grade students more leniently than another teacher. Grade inflation may result in many students' receiving "A"s and "B"s without actual improvements in achievement.

"A divergence between grades from classroom teachers and scores on standardized tests," notes Evers, "can be a wake-up call for parents, taxpayers, and school boards—telling us that students don't really know the subject matter and that teachers are too soft in their grading practices. Getting rid of standardized tests is like getting rid of thermometers, X-ray machines, and blood-pressure gauges in a doctor's office" (Evers, 2001).

Although data from mass testing may jolt schools into the first stirrings of reform, problems undeniably accompany so-called high-stakes testing. There is, for instance, the political element: How high a rate of school failure is politically acceptable? When Virginia launched its Standards of Learning testing in 1998, for instance, fewer than 3 percent of public schools could meet the seemingly modest requirement that 70 percent of each school's students pass the tests of core-subject knowledge. The passing rate has climbed dramatically, but Virginia still faces the prospect of stripping accreditation from hundreds of its public schools, or lowering the standards it has been pushing the schools to achieve. Similarly, the complex formula for Title I testing in the version of federal reform being negotiated on Capitol Hill had Washington's policymakers puzzling in the summer of 2001 over just how many schools they could afford to fail. Moreover, the problem of failing schools pales in comparison to the problem of what to do when high numbers of students cannot pass end-of-course or graduation tests.

The bottom line is that high-stakes tests increase the likelihood of school officials and policymakers manipulating testing procedures to attain the results desired. Simply by excluding from the testing large numbers of disabled or limited-English-proficient children, a local district or a state may pad the scores and reap undeserved praise in the press. Another kind of unfairness occurs when scores from a school serving affluent families are compared straight up with scores from a school that serves children who've grown up in the poorest of neighborhoods.

A fair and objective system would identify the difference that schools and teachers make with the individual children they serve—the value that they add to each child's learning, so to speak, regardless of where that child started in school or what kind of advantages or disadvantages he or she brings to the classroom.

So-called value-added assessment holds much promise of being that method of testing. Properly refined, it could have its greatest impact on the quality of teaching in American K–12 schools—revolutionizing the way teachers are trained, hired, evaluated, retrained, rewarded, or encouraged to enter another line of work.

Speaking before the metropolitan school board in Nashville in January 2001, Tennessee statistician William Sanders rattled the education establishment when he disputed the connection commonly made between poverty and low student performance. "Of all the factors we study—class size, ethnicity, location, poverty—they all pale to triviality in the face of teacher effectiveness" (Long and Cass, 2001). Such a pronouncement rubbed against the grain of doctrine instilled in many educators during their training and retraining. As the perceptive education historian Diane Ravitch has documented, the dominant education progressivists long have maintained that many children shouldn't be pushed to absorb knowledge beyond their limited innate capacities; that they are better off with teachers who help them get in touch with their feelings and find a socially useful niche (Ravitch, 2000). But teaching matters. It matters a lot (Haycock, 1998).

Sanders wasn't just being contrarian for the sake of being contrarian. He had more than a decade and a half of research in identifying the difference that teaching makes to back up his assertion. In 1983, when Tennessee first ventured into legislated education reform by emphasizing basic skills and a version of merit pay for teachers, Sanders and a colleague (Robert A. McLean) at the University of Tennessee began independently exploring the feasibility of employing a statistical mixed-model methodology to overcome the usual problems in using student achievement as an instrument of assessment—problems such as transient students, missing records, shifting teacher assignments, and the blurring of individual input with team teaching (Sanders and Horn, 1994).

The Tennesseans drew on volumes of student achievement data from Knox County to build a statistical tool of analysis. They were able to detect measurable, consistent differences among teachers regarding their effect on student performance, and these did not seem to be predictable according to where the school was located. And under effective teachers, students could make gains no matter what their ability or achievement levels were when they started.

Why not, then, a system taking into account the value that each teacher added, no matter the starting point of his or her pupils? Why not value-added assessment? Thus, when the state of Tennessee went into its second phase of results-oriented education reform, the assessment system honed by Sanders and McLean was ready for prime time. With the enactment of the Education Improvement Act in 1991, the Tennessee value-added assessment system (TVASS) gained a key role in analyzing data on how public education was doing its primary job of raising student achievement.

Basically, TVAAS works like this:

- Each spring, students take the norm-referenced state tests—a customized version of McGraw-Hill's Terra Nova test—in five core subjects (math, science, reading, language, and social studies). Fresh, nonredundant test items are added each year in an attempt to discourage blatant "teaching to the test."
- Each fall, districts receive a report card broken down by school and grade, showing progress in each subject in the context of three-year averages The system records student achievement gains in scale score points and in the form of comparisons to local, state, and national averages. School and district reports are released to the public.
- Each teacher receives a report card—one that is *not* released to the general public—showing the year-to-year progress of his or her students. Supervisors also receive these reports. It is this application of these data that holds the greatest promise for building a better teacher.

Table 8.1 presents a portion of an actual TVAAS report for an individual teacher in a recent year. The Tennessee system expresses achievement gains in scale score points, and renders comparisons of local, state, and national averages. In the sample teacher report, the teacher has produced gains that are impressive in language and science, but less so in math. The data help shed light on where improvement is needed.

John Stone, founder of the online Education Consumers Clearinghouse and that rare education professor who is also a keen critic of the government K–12 monopoly, points out that value-added assessment could be used by education's decision-makers "to isolate and assess the effectiveness of everything from the latest curricular innovations, to the preparedness of novice teachers, to the quality of the programs in which teachers were trained" (Stone, 1999).

Two specialists in teacher evaluation, James H. Stronge and Pamela D. Tucker, believe that using this sophisticated form of statistical

Table 8.1
Estimated Mean Gains (in Parentheses) and Their Standard Errors

| Estimated Mean Gains and (in parenthesis) their Standard Errors | | | | | |
|---|---|---|---|---|---|
| | Math | Reading | Language | Social St. | Science |
| USA Norm Gain | 26.0 | 21.0 | 11.0 | 22.0 | 19.0 |
| State Mean Gain | 25.0 | 20.4 | 19.3 | 21.4 | 21.4 |
| | | | | | |
| 1995 Teacher Gain | 22.7 (4.8) | 24.0 (3.8) | 22.3 (4.2) | 30.6 (4.9) | 28.3 (4.1) |
| 1995 System Gain | 12.3 (2.9) | 22.5 (3.4) | 19.8 (3.0) | 27.9 (3.8) | 27.5 (3.1) |
| | | | | | |
| 1996 Teacher Gain | 33.3 (4.9) | 28.5 (4.0) | 28.4 (3.8) | 18.3 (5.8) | 26.8 (4.0) |
| 1996 System Gain | 32.6 (3.0) | 28.6 (3.6) | 29.5 (3.2) | 17.4 (4.0) | 28.3 (3.3) |
| | | | | | |
| 1997 Teacher Gain | 15.6 (5.7) | 18.7 (4.9) | 17.8 (4.9) | 17.9 (5.7) | 25.6 (4.5) |
| 1997 System Gain | 16.3 (3.1) | 19.1 (3.6) | 16.0 (3.2) | 18.1 (4.0) | 26.1 (3.3) |
| | | | | | |
| Teacher 3-Yr-Avg | 23.9 (3.0) | 23.7 (2.5) | 22.8 (2.5) | 22.3 (3.2) | 26.9 (2.4) |
| System 3-Yr Avg | 20.4 (1.7) | 23.4 (2.0) | 21.8 (1.8) | 21.1 (2.3) | 27.3 (1.9) |
| | | | | | |
| Teacher 3-Year-Average Gain Comparisons | | | | | |
| Teacher vs. Norm: | NDD from Norm | NDD from Norm | Above Norm | NDD from Norm | Above Norm |
| Teacher vs. State: | NDD from Mean | NDD from Mean | NDD from Mean | NDD from Mean | Above Mean |
| Teacher vs. System: | NDD from Mean | NDD from Mean | NDD from Mean | NDD from Mean | NDD from Mean |

*Note*: NDD stands for "not detectably different."

analysis of year-to-year student achievement gains is a more accurate way to identify good teachers than the praxis exams for entering teachers (Stronge and Tucker, 2001). Praxis I measures a teacher's basic reading, writing, and math skills. Praxis may usefully screen out near-illiterates from teaching, but what about the creative teacher who inspires students despite falling a few points below math passing? Should such a teacher be able to prove his or her mettle through an on-the-job value-added analysis?

Two value-added models have evolved since the 1990s. One, used at the district level in Dallas, compares student growth to that of other students with similar socioeconomic characteristics (Kanstoroom, 2000). In contrast, TVAAS compares each student's test-score gains to his or her own previous growth rate while trying to weed out any influence of extraneous factors. Stronge and Tucker contend that TVAAS is "conceptually the simpler and more accurate" of the two models. Marci Kanstoroom of the Thomas B. Fordham Foundation says that whether to incorporate the confounding factors of student background into the mix is "a charged and complicated question." Those who favor the Dallas model contend that socioeconomic background affects not only where students begin, but how much progress they make from year to year. Low-income and minority students will make less progress over time. But William Sanders argues that "student background is not strongly correlated with gains a student will make, once the student's test scores in previous years are taken into account." Sanders' view is that the quality of teaching trumps the other factors.

This is seemingly a question to make policy wonks scratch their heads: Is omitting socioeconomic variables unfair to schools or teachers with high proportions of disadvantaged students? Or does taking these into account actually suggest lower expectations—the "soft bigotry of low expectations" decried by George W. Bush in his presidential campaign—that poor and minority students aren't really expected to raise their achievement as much as others? That is, do educators too often harm poor and minority students by failing to expect as much academic progress from them as from more privileged children?

Actually, both the Sanders "mixed-model" version of value-added analysis and the Dallas system, based on a statistical technique called "regression analysis" that is more familiar to education researchers, take socioeconomic status (SES) into account. They just do so differently. The Sanders model is conceptually simpler and geared more to the individual than to group identification. TVAAS effectively compares each student's annual scores with his or her scores over the past several years—scores that have been affected by whatever SES, IQ, genetic, motivational, or other conditions influenced the individual during that period. Thus, it takes into account not only SES but other factors that have influenced achievement over time. The Dallas approach, by contrast, attempts to ensure fair assessments of gain by comparing scores of individual members of a given SES group (such as black, urban, low-income) not against their own prior performance but against a mark adjusted by the average performance for their "group."

Undoubtedly, more value-added research worthy of peer-reviewed publication is in order. In quest of the highest degree of statistical accuracy, there could be variations or hybrids of the current methods. But the Sanders and TVAAS models appear to be more in tune with the ideal of individualism, as opposed to group stereotypes and entitlements.

School and accountability systems could use the value-added approach primarily in a diagnostic rather than a punitive way, to help weak teachers rather than suddenly imposing arbitrary standards. In addition, value-added comparisons could yield valuable consumer information to help parents know how well their schools are helping their children improve, and even enabling them to make choices among competing schools.

Bill Sanders believes the worst of all possible uses for test data is the simple reporting of raw test data, as newspapers often have done. Socioeconomic factors confound the straight use of such data. "Students within a school, serving primarily a low socio-economic community, could be making wonderful academic progress, yet their average test scores could be considerably lower than the district's average, leaving the erroneous impression that this is a woefully ineffective school. Students from another school, serving a population from more advantaged homes, could be 'sliding' and 'gliding,' nevertheless leaving the naïve impression that this second school is 'better' than the first because its average test scores are higher than the first school" (Sanders, 2000: 332).

This may be one of the most overlooked problems of modern education. Well-to-do families may conclude their children are receiving superb instruction because their norm-referenced test scores are relatively high. Yet, many of those young persons may be coasting and accomplishing little or nothing. Because schools fail to challenge them, they don't have to study, and find themselves with lots of time on their hands. If constructive activities like sports or part-time jobs fail to fill the void, they may entertain themselves with destructive activities.

Models that attempt to take socioeconomic factors into account through the use of such "predictors" as ethnicity or the percentage of students eligible for free or reduced-price school lunches are a "vast improvement" over use of raw test data, Sanders believes. Yet he has serious qualms about such an approach. Using such numbers to leaven raw data, he believes, could unintentionally encourage a lowering of expectations for youngsters who come from disadvantaged backgrounds. Achievement gains come from urban housing projects, the hollows of Appalachia, and millionaires' homes alike, even though the proportions of high achievers may not be the same from each segment of society. Hence, he strongly believes that the best method of evaluation simply uses each student as his or her own "control," focusing on the academic improvement that each child makes over time (Sanders and Horn, 1994). Thereby value-added provides a way to diagnose individual learning problems and to isolate the impact of teaching, so that a good teacher's work may be rewarded and an inadequate teacher's flaws may be corrected.

Plainly, good teaching matters. (Unfortunately, poor teaching also has a profound impact.) Sanders and other researchers have found that students unlucky enough to have a succession of poor teachers are virtually doomed to the education cellar. Three consecutive years of 1st quintile (least effective) teachers in grades 3 to 5 yield math scores from the 35th to the 45th percentile. Conversely, three straight years of 5th quintile teachers result in scores at the 85th to 95th percentile. Put another way, students with three straight years of effective teachers had 60 percent greater achievement than those unfortunate enough to have a succession of ineffective teachers (Stronge and Tucker, 2001). Having a string of ineffective teachers for three years can essentially ruin a child's chances of succeeding in school. Figure 8.1 reveals that students assigned ineffective teachers three years running score more than 50 percentile points below their peers who were lucky enough to be assigned highly effective teachers three years in a row. To avert the damage wreaked by back-to-back-to-back poor teachers, Sanders advocates building a "teacher assignment sequence" into school planning to the effect that no student has an ineffective teacher more than once. (Even better, of course, would be an assurance that students *never* encountered an ineffective teacher, though that ideal may never be reached.)

Within school systems, perhaps the greatest boon of value-added assessment is to teachers who do a superior job of helping low-achieving students. Often they labor in obscurity now, their work unappreciated or even denigrated by lack of public understanding of the difficult challenges they face. By focusing on gains, value-added assessment can identify good teachers who are successful with low achievers as well as poor teachers who permit high achievers to coast. Fair comparisons could help students at the low and high ends of the achievement spectrum, while helping teachers, too.

The "No Excuses" schools identified by an ongoing Heritage Foundation project—high-poverty schools where outstanding pupil achievement defies stereotypes about race and poverty—bolster Sanders' contention that teaching matters. Consider, for instance, Frederick Douglass Academy, a public school in central Harlem that has a student population 80 percent black and 19 percent Hispanic. The *New York Times* recently reported that all of Frederick Douglass' students passed a new, rigorous English Regents exam, and 96 percent passed

**Figure 8.1**
**Cumulative Effects of Teacher Sequence on Fifth Grade Math Scores for Two Metropolitan Systems**

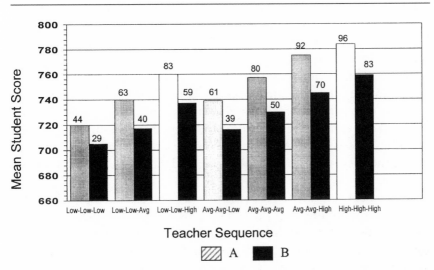

*Note*: Numbers above columns denote the corresponding percentile (CTB/McGraw-Hill, 1990: 104–115). Reprinted with permission from the University of Tennessee Value-Added Research and Assessment Center.

the math Regents. The grades 6–12 school ranks among the top ten schools in New York City in reading and math, despite having class sizes of 30 to 34. What makes the difference?

"Committed teachers," said principal Gregory M. Hodge—teachers, he said, who come to work early, stay late, and call parents if children don't show up for extra tutoring. The disciplined yet caring climate for learning set by Hodge and principals of other No Excuses schools also is due much credit.

In building better teachers such as those at Frederick Douglass Academy, the value-added approach recognizes the transforming potential of individual differences as opposed to one-size-fits-all standards.

"I believe we should visualize the curriculum not as stair steps, but rather as a ramp," Bill Sanders asserts (Hill, 2000). "I want all kids to go up the ramp but I recognize that not all kids are going to be at the same place at the same time. What I want us to hold educators accountable for is the speed of movement up the ramp, not the position on the ramp."

Adds Sanders: "Society has a right to expect that schools will provide students with the opportunity for academic gain regardless of the level at which the students enter the educational venue. In other words, all students can and should learn commensurate with their abilities" (Hill, 2000).

To be sure, value-added assessment has its critics: Some of them complain that the statistical analysis is too complicated. Some say teaching entails too many intangibles to be quantified. Knee-jerk opponents of standardized testing object to using norm-referenced, multiple-choice tests. And what about learning that takes place at home, they ask. Not all a child's gains or deficits can be attributed to a teacher.

Sanders concedes that "there is no way you can measure all of the important things a teacher does in the classroom." But, he adds, "that doesn't mean you shouldn't be measuring the things that can be measured" (Hill, 2000). No doubt family does influence a student's learning, but unless there are severe disruptions, such as serious illness, the influence of home tends to be a constant that would not negate value-added assessments of a teacher's impact on learning.

Value-added assessment holds the promise of being one important tool in the building of a better teacher for American schools.

# CHAPTER 9

# *Free-Agent Teachers*

Bad ideas sometimes die slowly. The notion that governmental regulators must dominate the education of children has passed away more gradually in the United States than in most other Western democracies. Denmark began subsidizing parental choice of private schools in 1899. Sweden, Holland, New Zealand, and Australia are among other industrialized countries that have embraced and subsidized private choice (Andrews, 2002).

With the dawn of a new century, the monopoly finally is beginning to crack in the United States. As education begins to become a freer market, the implications for teaching will be profound.

Perhaps the biggest break, the one with historical gravity, came when Wall Street entrepreneur Theodore J. Forstmann and Wal-Mart director John Walton joined in forming the Children's Scholarship Fund (CSF) in September 1998 with the intent of funding 40,000 K–12 scholarships for the nation's neediest children. Together, they donated $100 million, and with the help of a diverse, bipartisan board of distinguished Americans, they raised another $70 million. The aid they offered nationwide took the form of partial scholarships to enable needy children to attend schools of their choice. To be eligible, families had to earn less than $22,000 per year, and had to agree to chip in an average of $1,000 per year to supplement their children's scholarships. That is a considerable investment for low-income parents to replace a product they already receive "free" from the government. So big was this requested commitment, indeed, that the philanthropists did not know what sort of a response they could expect.

The response was staggering: CSF received 1.25 million applications for the 40,000 scholarships. Demand was especially high in the central cities. In Baltimore, 44 percent of eligible families applied; in Washington, D.C., 33 percent; in New York City, 29 percent; and in Chicago, 26 percent. On April 21, 1999, CSF had to conduct a national lottery to distribute the scholarships. Forstmann may well be proven right in his prediction that National Lottery Day will be remembered as a turning point in the history of American education.

"The parents of 1.25 million children put an end to the debate over whether low-income families want choice in education: They passionately, desperately, unequivocally do," noted Forstmann at a national leadership seminar sponsored by Hillsdale College. "Now it is up to the defenders of the *status quo* to tell them, and the millions they represent, why they cannot have it" (Forstmann, 1999: 2).

Choice and competition are challenging the status quo on many fronts now. On June 27, 2002, the U.S. Supreme Court issued a monumental decision in a Cleveland case upholding the constitutionality of publicly funded scholarships (vouchers) that enable low-income families to choose better schools for their kids, even if the schools are religiously oriented (*Zelman*, 2002). By the following April, Colorado had enacted a statewide voucher program for needy children, joining the voucher parade that began in Milwaukee and expanded to Cleveland and Florida in the years before the landmark High Court decision. Furthermore, key Democratic officials in the District of Columbia, led by Mayor Anthony Williams, were throwing their support behind federally funded vouchers that would be part of a broad strategy for uplifting education in the nation's capital. In addition, over the past 15 years a half-dozen states have adopted either general education tax credits or tuition tax credits for individuals, corporations, or organizations using their money to advance private choice in education. In the wake of the Supreme Court's affirmation of school choice as a reform strategy, many more states and the federal government were considering following suit.

A more direct form of school choice is embodied in the phenomenal rise of home schooling. Brian Ray, who heads the National Home Education Research Institute and has been doing widely respected studies of home schooling since the 1980s, estimates that in the fall of 2001 between 1.6 million and 2 million children were being home-schooled in the United States. Of that number, he estimated that 5 percent are African-Americans. Even though precise figures are lacking, many signs point to a surge of black participation in the home-schooling movement. Given that blacks have been a core constituency for public education (having had to wage a civil rights revolution to gain equal access), the beginnings of a movement toward home schooling by black parents is one of the strongest signs of a broad-based demand for educational freedom. Ray commented that from a little research and a good deal of traveling the country and meeting with home educators, he concludes that "African-American home schooling is growing and growing fast" (Holland, 2002).

The growth of competitive education also is rising, to some extent, within the system—in the form of charter schools. Public charter schools, which gain a degree of independence from the central bureaucracy in return for a contractual promise to be accountable for academic results, may have achieved a critical mass that will enable them to change the face of American public education permanently. Just a decade after the first such innovative public school opened in Minnesota in 1991, more than 2,500 public charter schools were in operation nationwide. Where charter schools exist, both parents and teachers have the power to choose them; indeed, teachers and parents often are instrumental in founding charter schools. To be sure, the gains are not coming without nasty rearguard resistance, sometimes amounting to dirty tricks, from public-school bureaucracies fearful of competition (Scarborough, 2001). One of the features of the most independent charter schools most hated by the status-quo-loving education establishment is the ability of these schools to hire teachers from outside the standard ed-school track.

With the opening of classes in the fall of 2002, Philadelphia embarked on the boldest venture yet in privatization of failing public schools. Edison Schools and other private providers are running 70 of the city's most troubled schools under the watchful eye of a School Reform Commission jointly appointed by the governor of Pennsylvania and the mayor of Philadelphia. While the depth of the system's academic and fiscal problems cried out for bold action, the state takeover faces fierce opposition from teacher unions and many local community groups and politicians. It is at best a venture in quasi-privatization, with the government still a player in the background and politics sure to be a constant companion. Edison received 20 schools to manage (it had sought 45), and other private managers run an additional 22. The remaining troubled schools became charter schools, independent schools managed by teachers and parents, or reconstituted public schools with new staffs. The commission can fire school managers if their students' scores fall below the pre-takeover levels (Dean and Brennan, 2002). This represents far more accountability than ever existed for Philly's conventional public schools. However, even some market-oriented reformers believe the Philly approach basically just swaps a government school monopoly for a privatized school monopoly rather than truly putting clout in the hands of education consumers (Brouillette, 2001).

Whatever happens in Philadelphia, education companies, or "edupreneurs," are likely to surge elsewhere. Carrie Lips, a former policy analyst at the Cato Institute, has noted that this rapidly expanding industry already constitutes 10 percent of the $740 billion education market. They are demonstrating, she said, that "even when competing against a monopolistic system, [they] can deliver a wide range of affordable high-quality educational services." Education tax credits that return purchasing power to individuals could further loosen the grip of the government monopoly "and allow the natural growth of a vibrant educational marketplace" (Lips, 2000).

One government action that could provide a stimulus to privatization is the "supplemental services" provision in the reform of federal aid to education that President George W. Bush and such congressional leaders as Senator Ted Kennedy hammered out on a bipartisan basis. The No Child Left Behind Act of 2001 will allow parents whose children are stuck in chronically failing schools to take up to $1,000 per child of their federal subsidy out of the schools and use it for hiring a private tutor. Although tuition vouchers didn't fly with Congress, the tutoring grants resemble remedial education vouchers. In the fall of 2002, the first round of these remedial vouchers promptly became available for patrons of 3,000 public schools already identified as failing under the 1994 version of the Elementary and Secondary Education Act.

This new form of subsidized parental choice figured to be a certain windfall for established tutorial companies like Huntington Learning Centers, Kaplan, Inc., and Sylvan Learning Centers. In addition, the new law permits faith-based and other nonprofit organizations to become qualified tutorial providers under regulations the education bureaucrats will write (Walsh, 2002). Indicative of the ferment in this segment of the education industry, Sylvan Learning Systems, Inc. announced in March 2003 its intention to sell its K–12 operational units and to concentrate on its international and online university enterprises. As part of the divestiture, Educate, Inc. will own the Sylvan Learning Centers and other K–12 tutorial businesses. No matter the corporate banners, Sylvan and other providers no doubt will be major players in providing supplemental services to children ill-served by failing public schools.

Private providers are even making inroads on that most closely guarded bastion of the public education monopoly: teacher training. Sylvan acquired a major interest in online Walden University with the purpose of expanding training programs for teachers. Edison aspires to operating its own Teachers College with long-range plans for campuses in 20 cities. The 75,000-student University of Phoenix is another major supplier of private teacher training via the Internet.

The Internet is a powerful tool for edupreneurs. Cyber charter schools are on that new frontier: while conventional charter schools have a degree of autonomy from the local school bureaucracy, cyber charters take freedom out into the limitless ether by offering curricular choices that are available to anyone in the world. Moreover, home-schooling parents are forming co-ops that make extensive use of curricula available over the Internet. In the 1980s, a few thousand children took their school lessons at home; today, almost 2 million do. Teaching is becoming both globally transmittable and home-rooted.

By the year 2020, K–12 education in America may little resemble education in 2002. The emergence of education responsive to market demand will benefit consumers—children most of all.

The rise of a competitive education market also will bring profound changes for teachers and their preparation and opportunities. As we have seen, certification of the nation's schoolteachers over the past century has been largely in the hands of a like-thinking monolith centered around the professional schools of education and government education bureaucracies. This system has favored sameness over intellectual diversity.

Soon the opening of education markets should introduce teacher training to fresh perspectives. Two forces converging to challenge the status quo are (1) the drive to reform American K–12 education, embodied at the federal level in the No Child Left Behind Act of 2001, which places a premium on attracting and retaining the most knowledgeable teachers possible, from a variety of pathways, and (2) the presumed teacher shortage, which is more precisely a shortage of well-prepared teachers and teachers willing to tackle difficult challenges.

The immediate need to fill teaching jobs for an upcoming school year has caused many school administrators to weigh the benefits of hiring liberal arts graduates or people from the working world who have a demonstrated grasp of subjects like mathematics or history.

Those elements of the education establishment with a vested interest in preserving the current monopoly of labor in education (including the teacher unions) grouse that opening new routes to teaching amounts to lowering standards. "Whenever we have a large teacher shortage as we do right now," declared Kathleen Lyons of the National Education Association, "you will see that licensing and credentials are thrown out the window and warm bodies are simply placed in classrooms" (Coeyman, 2001). However, studies such as one conducted by Dominic Brewer of RAND and Dan Goldhaber of the Urban Institute have established that students taught with alternatively certified teachers perform every bit as well as students taught with fully certified teachers (Goldhaber and Brewer, 1999, 2000).

Alternative certification is being pursued largely through publicly funded programs, but by opening unconventional paths to teaching careers, it opens the door for greater privatization. Ultimately, the spread of school choice may be what spurs the entry of private enterprise into the closed world of teacher preparation. In response to parental demand for varied choices in educational styles, private educational companies—some nonprofit, some for-profit—are establishing beachheads in communities around the country. In addition, the public charter schools find it desirable to select (often from alternative paths) and train their own teachers who can implement the schools' distinctive styles of education. A survey of charter schools' personnel policies showed that teachers reap the rewards and shoulder the responsibilities of being freer agents than their peers in regular government schools. Almost half (46 percent) of the charter schools reported that they give merit pay—typically 5 to 10 percent of base pay—to their most productive teachers. At the same time, dismissals of teachers for poor performance are commonplace in charter schools, particularly those not under collective bargaining agreements (Podgursky and Ballou, 2001).

Among the nonprofits, the Core Knowledge (CK) Foundation, which was founded by cultural literacy advocate E. D. Hirsch, Jr., has begun developing grade-by-grade handbooks for its teachers, along the lines of "What the Third Grade Teacher Needs to Know." CK also has subject-matter syllabi that it uses in pre-service and in-service courses for its teachers. Hirsch is a critic of the dominant view in ed-school circles that teachers should be mere facilitators of student-directed learning rather than transmitters of knowledge. Hence, CK finds itself increasingly in the business of preparing teachers and principals.

An outstanding example of how CK helps teachers with depth of understanding of curricular content is the series of texts and guidebooks in history and geography for early grades that CK and the Pearson Learning Group jointly issued in mid-2002. A key precept of the CK approach is that learning is a cumulative process—knowledge builds on knowledge. Understanding of mathematics begins in kindergarten, and instruction continues every year. However, Hirsh noted in a letter announcing the CK/Pearson guides that "in recent times we have neglected a similar truth about learning history. Knowledge of history that has shaped our country and our world should be fostered early so that it will grow and deepen over time." (Indeed, many college students—future teachers included—can take their degrees from modern American universities without having had so much as one history course.)

The series of CK/Pearson books covers progressively more complex topics, from exploring and settling America and Mount Rushmore presidents for kindergarten, to such early civilizations as Mesopotamia and ancient Egypt in the first grade, to ancient Greece, making the (U.S.) Constitution, and the Civil War (among other topics) in the second grade. For each period of history taught, there is a detailed teacher guide to help teachers introduce a lesson with background information, provoke class discussion, present key vocabulary words with clear definitions to increase comprehension, make cross-curricular connections (e.g., relating Civil War history to science by noting how cotton was cultivated), engaging students in activities to enrich their learning, and conducting a thorough review with discussion to assess students' grasp of the material.

Edison Schools, the largest for-profit manager of public schools, has envisioned an even more ambitious venture in private teacher training, one that could make it "the nation's largest operator of teachers' colleges" (Symonds, 2001). The company announced plans for an entire division—Edison Teachers Colleges—and initially put in charge of it former Detroit school superintendent Deborah McGriff, who led Edison's charter-school development. "We're responding to our [school district and charter school] partners who say there is much to be gained in terms of improving the quality of teachers," McGriff said when Edison announced in May 2000 that it would be researching the best way to launch its own teachers colleges (Walsh, 2000).

Edison has been slow to achieve its goals of profitability. By mid-2003, the company had put the launch of its Teachers College on hold while "reengineering our business model." However, if Edison succeeds in its overall plan to become a major player in public education, the concept of private teacher training will receive a big boost. Edison plans to guarantee all its successful trainees teaching jobs, although they will be free to teach elsewhere.

Asked by a Lexington Institute researcher why Edison contemplated such an ambitious plan, McGriff replied, "To ensure that we have the quantity of teachers and administrators needed to meet our growth targets and the talent needed to meet our academic performance targets."

Asked if there was a perception that existing schools of education are not turning out enough well-prepared teachers, she responded, diplomatically, "There is a national teacher shortage and teachers do not feel well prepared." McGriff added that "our [Edison's] curriculum will integrate theory and practice. Each course will have a clinical component. Our graduates will close the achievement gap."

Another significant development has been Sylvan's quiet entry into teacher training. Sylvan hasn't evinced interest in setting up its own teachers college, but instead has been contracting with individual school districts to provide what they need to bring their uncertified teachers up to acceptable standards.

Seeking to fill a critical need for well-qualified K–12 teachers, Sylvan began its first teacher training programs in the fall of 2000. Much of the course work is offered online. In addition, Sylvan has assigned "instructional managers"—mainly retired educators—to groups of 25 teachers in training (Bradley, 2000).

In Texas, Sylvan has worked with school districts that produce one-fourth of the state's new teachers through their own licensure systems. It has an eye on helping in particular those working on emergency certificates or long-term substitute teachers.

Recently Sylvan's clout as a trainer of teachers took a quantum leap forward with its investment of $32.8 million to acquire 41 percent ownership of Walden University, an institution based in Bonita Springs, Florida, and Minneapolis that has pioneered in distance and online learning for working adults who seek graduate degrees. Sylvan brings to relatively small Walden the name recognition it earned from helping lagging K–12 students catch up, and Walden brings to the partnership its full accreditation from the North Central Association of Colleges and Schools, which opens e-students' access to federal financial aid. A third partner is another Sylvan investment, Canter and Associates, which already had developed with Walden a new specialization in elementary reading and literacy as part of the university's master's degree program in education.

Market analysts said Walden's online expertise, combined with Sylvan's credible move to fill a huge void in teacher preparation, makes for extraordinary growth potential. "Walden clearly has a good model," noted Adam Newman, senior analyst with Eduventures.com. "It's accredited. It has the infrastructure in place. It understands the distance-learning postsecondary market. The merger could end up being more about how to use Walden to grow Sylvan" (Office.com, 2001).

Yet another partnership Sylvan has entered—this one with Teachers College, Columbia University—underscores the point that the company aspires to work within the education establishment, not to challenge it head-on. Teachers College is the granddaddy of U.S. schools of education, and the single institution most influencing such schools to steep would-be teachers in the child-centered or constructivist methodology, as opposed to teacher-directed instruction in the basics. According to a June 2000 announcement, Sylvan will work with Teachers College in preparing teachers to win certification from the National Board for Professional Teaching Standards (NBPTS).

The release touted NBPTS, a creation of the Carnegie Corporation that is now federally funded, as "highly selective" and "rigorous" (Caliber.com, 2001). As noted in chapter 5, critics and advocates of objectively measured teacher-centered instruction strongly disagree.

Teachers College will provide course content and instruction for the Internet-delivered NBPTS prep course. Sylvan will concentrate on supporting on-site mentors and working with local school districts.

The 75,000-student University of Phoenix, the nation's largest for-profit university and another pioneer in online instruction, is also bidding to make a large impact on teacher training. Its College of Education, with 1,200 undergraduates and 3,500 master's degree enrollees, is, like Sylvan, seeking to cooperate with the teacher-education establishment. It has received approval from several states to offer programs to prepare teachers hired on a temporary basis for full licensure. In addition, Phoenix has been negotiating for membership with the gatekeepers to teaching—the National Council for Accreditation of Teacher Education and the American Association of Colleges for Teacher Education. The latter organization recently accepted Phoenix into its fold.

All this has caused a degree of consternation in the ed-school community, where some pedagogues deem "profit" a dirty word. But Allen Glenn, Dean Emeritus of the University of Washington's College of Education and chairman of a task force that studied private teacher training, sees potential benefits in the diversification:

"When people have choices, competition and service become instrumental," Glenn commented in a July 25, 2001, E-mail to this author. "Colleges of education are now just one choice among many for education. Competition will only escalate."

As private providers become more and more of a force in training teachers, it is logical to assume that the field will open to divergent educational philosophies and operate less like an entrenched monopoly. As that happens, the benefits of increased educational freedom in the United States could finally extend to the classroom teacher, the person whose work is so crucial to academic progress.

Thoughtful teachers seem to understand the potential benefits of greater choice of various kinds. Here are the thoughts of some of them who responded to a survey done for this book:

Camille Farrington is in her second year of teaching at the Young Women's Leadership Charter School (YWLCS) in the inner city of Chicago. Prior to that, she taught for eight years in regular public schools of Oakland, California, and Madison, Wisconsin. YWLCS—specializing in mathematics, science, and technology—is one of only four public all-girls schools in the United States. A group of attorneys and business leaders proposed and organized the charter school as a way to address the "gender imbalances" in professions requiring scientific, mathematical, or technical expertise. Farrington, who is certified in English and history, teaches humanities within a curriculum that has a higher degree of math and science than do the regular schools.

She likes the fact that the school has a clearly stated mission and vision, and teachers as well as families are there because they bought into that design.

"The thing I love," she said, "is that if you have an idea, and it's sound pedagogically and you can argue it persuasively, there's nothing standing between you and carrying it out. The administration and the board of directors are really supportive of teachers."

Illinois law is flexible enough to allow for diversity of background among charter school teachers. Teachers must have a college degree and either three years' teaching experience or three years' work experience in the content field. That is a help in recruiting math and science specialists, who are in short supply in public schools.

Joyce Clayton, a ten-year teaching veteran with a degree in the social sciences, came to her current secondary school in Lakeland, Florida, in 1995 when it opened as a public school of choice. In 1998, it converted to a charter school—McKeel Academy of Technology. Before coming to McKeel, she had taught sixth grade in a traditional middle school.

> I feel that I have more freedom, not only in the classroom, but in how the administration schedules classes. We are able to manipulate the schedule to accommodate the students' needs because we control our funding for teachers. We are also able to limit our class sizes, which creates a more conducive learning environment and gives teachers the opportunity to teach outside the box—different from traditional teaching methods.
>
> Both the mission and vision statement were created by the entire faculty. The process made us look at what we want our graduates to "look like"—what skills we want them to possess, abilities they need to succeed, and knowledge they will need to be competitive beyond high school.

McKeel uses a technology-based curriculum in grades 6–12. The curriculum is centered around "real-life experiences and an integrated approach to learning."

Concerning teacher influence, Clayton elaborated as follows:

> The teaching staff works in academic teams to better serve the needs of our students. Each team has a . . . manager who meets weekly with the school director and administrative staff to discuss needs, problems, and concerns. This group is a decision-making group that also offers suggestions to administrators as to the needs of classroom teachers. The group also is responsible for approving expenses for team members, maintaining a team budget, and dispersing information from the team

manager meetings to their team. This position would be somewhat equivalent to middle management in the corporate world.

McKeel also has a performance-based system of pay, pegged in part to 90 percent of students increasing their achievement at least one level on the Florida Comprehensive Assessment Test. Other criteria include implementing Individualized Education Programs (IEPs), attending all in-service training, participating in ten extracurricular activities during the year, implementing a behavior management system, and successfully using the school's technology.

"Yes, I certainly do plan to continue my teaching career in a charter school," Clayton said in response to the questionnaire. "I have visited traditionally funded and taught schools, as well as having taught in them, and I know that teachers have a lot more input into how a charter is run and have more money for technology and classroom materials. In short, charter schools are what is best for students."

Roberta Williams teaches third grade in Corry, Pennsylvania, a rural community in the northwestern part of the state. She has been teaching full-time for 16 years and had taught kindergarten, first grade, a multiage class, and language arts prior to her current assignment. She also was a substitute teacher for 13 years while rearing her children. She has a master's degree in early childhood education. These are her thoughts on freedom of choice for teachers:

> Changing buildings and positions within my district has been a positive situation for me. A new situation allows for professional growth by providing a new set of experiences: different curriculum levels and age of children, change in teaching staff and building. Sometimes a teacher understands students' learning better by knowing where the student comes from (in prior grade levels). There is also a benefit from changing positions to prevent burnout, or in leaving a particular situation that was stressful for any number of reasons.
>
> However, the downside is that sometimes teachers have no choice, but are simply moved without reason. This contributes to low morale and other negative feelings—and seems to be happening with more frequency in our district.

Asked about teachers' having expanded choices among public charter schools or private options such as home-school co-ops, she replied:

> I am in favor of these opportunities. Teachers bring an enormous array of talents, teaching styles, philosophies, personalities, etc. However,

many of us feel as though we are being called to "standardize" everything. Making us all uniform squelches our creativity and all that we bring as individuals to the classroom.

As a parent of five children, one foster child, and four stepchildren, I am very aware that our present education system does not answer the need[s] of all children and in fact does more harm than good to some.

There is definitely a need for education to open the door to more alternatives. Both children and teachers would benefit. Teachers could make use of their varied talents and children might find more in schools that is meaningful to them. Another facet of this would be allowing teachers more flexibility in their job, [including] job-sharing, or part-time work.

Sara Matthews has been teaching for 20 years, with an occasional break to stay home with her children. She has taught at every level from preschool to college. For the past seven years, she has taught grades 5–8 in a school located in the suburbs of Philadelphia. Here's what she had to say about greater choice for teachers:

> I see each school as having a personality—even though we often try to hide that or deny it. Some teachers who are not right for my school would be right for another and vice versa. If teachers had greater choices—and if those choices were informed—they might find a better match and each of our schools might be able to achieve a great sense of themselves.
>
> It's also true that teaching is too isolated a profession. Teachers become convinced that their way is the only way or that their school's way is the only way. Teachers become entrenched, and that in a profession where flexibility is one of the keys to success. Moving between schools would theoretically allow for greater movement of ideas and a freshening of the stale culture that is too often teaching.

As for an economic benefit for teachers from choice, Mathews was less certain. "From what I see, there are so many teachers available that the supply well outweighs the demand. Teachers having greater choice between schools could theoretically, I suppose, create a greater demand for the good teachers but not for all teachers. We're too easy to replace, and with someone who'll work cheaper."

Don Verkow is an assistant principal at Paramount Charter Academy (an affiliate of National Heritage Academies) in Kalamazoo, Michigan. Before joining the front office, he had taught three years at Paramount. Education is a second career for Verkow, who spent 28 years in the private sector, mainly in supervisory positions in manufacturing. His wife, Katie, has taught in public charter schools and currently teaches in a parochial school. Verkow has substituted in public and private schools, and his two children have gone to both public and private schools. Given the eclectic nature of his family's educational experiences, Verkow believes he has an outlook on choice that differs from many public educators' view.

This is his take on teachers and choice:

> From our perspective, we have met a large number of teachers who have opted out of traditional public education to start over in a new setting. The main goal of these individuals was to be able to teach in an environment that supports the teacher's right to teach. In our own organization are a number of previously retired teachers and administrators who have enlisted in the cause of education reform. These folks are excited about working among educators who are more concerned with responsibly educating children than about adding to their retirement benefits; more enthusiastic about instructional innovation than union PAC rallies.
>
> Understand that while some charter school and private school teachers only accept a position as a temporary teaching job, many—if not most— are truly trying to make a difference. These professionals also accept that the pay in school is, of necessity, lower, and will probably always be so.
>
> The economic benefit will be to society in general, in terms of a better-prepared workforce coming from choice schools. Those who choose to teach in choice schools will never be paid on the same level as union teachers. Educating and adequately preparing children as life-long learners (not the accumulation of wealth and benefits) is the overriding concern in the choice teaching community.

To be sure, the idea of schools being part of a competitive market is anathema to many in public education. A teacher in northern California (who preferred that her name not be used) was concerned about the use of the word *competitive*.

> *Competitive* implies that there are winners and losers (as in sports) or superior and inferior (as in business). *Competitive* works well in sports and business because the inferior usually drop out. In our society today, there is no room for students who have not been successful in school. There was a time in our country when students who didn't achieve at school dropped out. It was a solution. They worked on a farm or did manual labor, and were able to support themselves and their families. This is no longer true. We don't have jobs like these in our country anymore. All students must be educated so that they have choices

among the jobs that are available. I worry when I hear about competitive schools. There is no room in our society for superior and inferior schools. All children deserve a superior school.

There are also those who seem to think that a competitive school system will inspire school employees to work harder and do better. I've yet to encounter a system that isn't already trying to do their best. I doubt that competition will inspire them to do more.

Tom Shuford, now retired in Ventura, California, after a 28-year teaching career, believes young teachers especially could benefit from choice, if they were more aware of market operations. He says his last salary in 1999 was on Long Island's North Shore, where with an M.A. plus 60 credits he commanded an $85,000 salary "with, of course, undreamed-of-in-the-private-sector job security, a great pension, health insurance, death benefit, dental plan." (Shuford worked in special education at the elementary-school level.)

He added:

In my well-off small district, there were about 300 applicants for every opening. The benefits of a freer market on Long Island would be for the many young, energetic teachers (and alternatively educated people) who want to teach but don't have the interview skills, three years' experience, good luck to land such a job.

I had many capable people, who worked a while for me as an assistant, leave because they could not get a start as a public-school teacher.

Freer markets mean many more options to the one-size-fits-all system for children, for parents, for young teachers, and for veterans with an entrepreneurial bent.

But for teachers already in the system, I think you will find few willing to risk such security for the uncertainty of the market. The pay and benefits disparity between public-school teachers and private-school teachers is well known.

On the whole, teachers surveyed thought greater job satisfaction—more than necessarily higher compensation—would be the benefit most expected to flow to teachers as a result of school choice. However, greater financial rewards could follow as teaching became a more attractive career for persons with much-in-demand skills and proven effectiveness.

Teachers in several Los Angeles schools expressed outrage recently when state bonuses intended to reward faculty whose schools made huge test-score gains were handed out strictly on the basis of teacher seniority.

Regardless of how hard individual teachers worked to pull up achievement at low-performing schools, the biggest bonuses went to teachers with the most years of service. Governor Gray Davis and the legislature had instituted the rewards for test-score gains at "challenged schools" on the hope that incentive would help attract and retain teachers to work in such schools. But when the Los Angeles teacher union refused to negotiate the size of the bonuses—citing its opposition to any pay being tied to test results—distribution of the money defaulted to a seniority-based formula.

The teacher outrage over seniority-based bonuses reported in the Los Angeles press was justifiable, but one wonders why teachers don't object more often to the standard method of compensation, which the teacher unions have insisted be scaled to seniority and college degrees rather than success in helping students achieve. "Even non-unionized districts tend to adopt salary scales that resemble union scales," Harvard scholar Caroline M. Hoxby has observed. "So teachers who excel at their jobs or teach hard-to-staff subjects, such as math and science, are paid the same as if they were mediocre or could be replaced easily" (Hoxby, 2001: 58).

Working in this highly regulated and standardized business, American teachers have had to settle for financial rewards that come nowhere close to matching the overall rates of increase in education spending. According to the U.S. Department of Education's National Center for Education Statistics, the average annual salary for public-school teachers in 1996–1997 was $38,509, which was less than one-third of the total dollars spent on public education.

There has been an explosion of spending for public education in recent decades, but classroom teachers have benefited not nearly as much as the bureaucrats who manage the government-controlled system. After adjusting for inflation, public-education spending has jumped 312 percent since 1959–1960. Yet teacher pay has gained only 43 percent after inflation since then. Clearly, the monolithic system rewards bureaucracy more than teaching. During this same period, the number of classroom teachers grew by 1.24 million while nonteaching personnel rose by over 1.66 million. Administrators, counselors, psychologists, and other support staff now account for almost half the salaried persons in U.S. public schools (Steidler, 1999).

The pay of public-school teachers exceeds that of private-school teachers by 51 percent, on average. That's because of private schools' competitive disadvantage: While they must run the school efficiently on tuition averaging a little over $3,000 per child, public schools receive well over double that per student in appropriations from the government and do not charge tuition. However, what's highly instructive is that numerous studies have shown that the lower-paid teachers in private schools have much higher levels of job satisfaction than do public-school teachers.

For instance, a survey by the research arm of the U.S. Department of Education found 52 percent of private-school teachers saying they certainly would become a teacher again, compared with just 38 percent of public-school teachers. A fifth of public-school teachers expressed "strong dissatisfaction" with their job, while only 8.9 percent of private-school teachers said they probably or certainly would not become a teacher had they the choice to make again (Steidler, 1999).

The Texas Public Policy Foundation looked at results of surveys of public school and private-school teachers in Texas in the late 1990s and found this situation:

- Just 40 percent of public-school teachers thought their school had improved during the past five years. About 75 percent of private-school teachers believed their school had improved.
- More than half of public-school teachers thought social promotion was a serious problem in their schools, while 29 percent of private-school teachers saw social promotion at problem levels.
- In response to the central question—*Are you seriously considering leaving the teaching profession?*—44 percent of public-school teachers said yes, versus 28 percent of private-school teachers.

Disciplinary headaches, the threat of violence, excessive paperwork, and an over-emphasis on testing are among causes of dissatisfaction that teachers often cite, in addition to relatively low pay. Are there ways to make teaching a more satisfying and rewarding line of work?

Parents in Ripton, Vermont, were uneasy at the prospect of their children moving from the town's small elementary school to a large, consolidated middle school in Middlebury. So they did something about it: They started their own one-room school. North Branch School now enrolls a dozen students aged 11 to 14.

The concern about public schools growing too large, to the point that children are anonymous at stages when they most need adult guidance, seems to be growing across Vermont, and perhaps the country as well. The Vermont Independent Schools Association reports that from 1981 to 1990, only 24 new private schools opened in the state. But from 1991 to 2000, Vermont saw the birth of 65 independent schools.

What's this got to do with teachers? Well, new schools need teachers, and there are teachers attracted to small schools where everything is on a human scale and everyone has a name instead of an ID number.

One of them is 36-year-old Tal Birdsey, who had attended a similar school in Atlanta and who has his bachelor's and master's degrees from Middlebury College.

"Personally, I want to be free," Birdsey said in an interview with an Associated Press reporter (Allen, 2001). "I look at teaching as an art, and as soon as someone tells you how to do art, it wrecks it."

Here is an example of how the exercise of parental choice can create a situation benefiting teachers—and, even more to the point, how enterprising teachers can use opportunities to make best use of their talents.

Harvard economist Caroline M. Hoxby believes that school choice could make teaching a more attractive career to persons who seek to work in a true profession where employees are rewarded not just on seniority but according to their talents and their ability to produce results. In the current system, teacher unions standardize wages so that teachers with the same length of service and same degrees usually receive the same salaries, no matter whether they are excellent, mediocre, or poor teachers. This is one reason teaching is not as attractive to persons of high aptitude, strong work habits, and math-science skills, says Hoxby. In particular, bright women with high aptitude have chosen management, law, and medicine over education because those professions do reward individuals according to their performance and abilities.

To test her theory that choice would make teaching more of a profession attracting the best and brightest, Hoxby looked at hiring practices in charter schools as well as localities where considerable choice existed among public schools via choice of residence. (The latter is called Tiebout choice, in recognition of economist Charles Tiebout, who called attention to its importance.) Where parents could choose charter schools, Hoxby compared teachers in the charters with those in private and regular public schools in the same regions.

In summary, what she found was that schools which face tougher competition for students face a demand to hire teachers who have graduated from colleges that are selective in admissions. (Many certified teachers come from colleges that are not very selective in admissions.) The need of charter and private schools to attract students in order to receive their funding seemingly drives their hiring of higher-aptitude teachers. Only 20 percent of regular public-school teachers attended competitive or selective colleges, contrasted with 36 percent of charter-school teachers and 36 percent of private-school teachers.

In addition, in areas where there was maximum Tiebout choice, a teacher was 15 percent more likely to have majored in math and science. A teacher in an area with a high level of private-school choice was 10 percent more likely to have majored in math or science. Furthermore, teachers who majored in math or science earned 16 percent more if they worked in areas with high degrees of school choice than they would have earned if they'd worked in communities with low levels of choice.

Schools that faced strong competition for students also were far more likely than regular public schools to hire teachers who had majored in an academic discipline, as opposed to professional education. In charter schools, 56 percent of teachers had majored in a field of the arts and sciences, compared with 37 percent of public-school teachers.

Another interesting finding was that charter-school teachers work 13 extra instructional hours per week, versus nine extra hours for the regular public-school teachers. But while charter-school teachers are paid an extra 5 percent for their work, the public-school teachers are not compensated for the extra work.

"Broadly speaking," Hoxby wrote, "my findings suggest that enhanced competition and choice raise the demand for high aptitude, skills in math and science, subject-area expertise, effort, and perhaps independence among teachers. Choice also seems to lower schools' demand for certification and master's degrees. These findings further suggest that school choice has the potential to create a professional environment for teachers in which more motivated and skilled teachers earn higher pay for such qualities."

Research conducted by Lexington Institute scholar Paul Steidler in 1999 established that while private schools have smaller classrooms than public schools, and lower-paid teachers, a much higher proportion of their education funds are directed toward teachers than is the case in the government-controlled schools. Using the most recent data then available, Steidler noted that teacher pay represents about 46.4 percent of total classroom revenues in private schools, compared with 32.9 percent of the total money going into public school classrooms. Of course, public-school overhead is far higher, with average revenues of $116,900 going into each classroom, compared with $46,740 per private classroom. These comparisons suggest the potential for market mechanisms that cut the overhead and ensure that more of the resources go to appropriate rewards for teachers.

The competition that flows from parental choice could serve as a catalyst to reduce bureaucratic costs and put teachers where they belong: at the center of operations. Were public schools as efficient as private schools, teacher pay could rise substantially as a result of a higher percentage of available dollars going to the classroom. Even more important, choice would attract motivated and broadly educated people into the profession. Teachers would be much freer to practice their art, and students would reap the benefits of being taught by people who were in the classrooms because they had chosen to be there.

To be sure, the value to teachers and to society of school choice is still largely in the realm of theory. But the case will become stronger as a competitive education industry continues to expand—with charter schools heading toward 3,000 nationwide, with new forms of choice like cyber charter schools coming online, with home schooling and home-school co-ops booming, and with enterprising parents and teachers like those in Vermont starting their own independent schools.

An increasingly free market in education can help in building those better teachers who contribute so mightily to the building of a better society.

# CHAPTER 10

## *Putting It All Together*

As a dedicated high school teacher might say before a final examination, let's review. But don't fret: There will be neither multiple-choice nor essay questions waiting for you at the end of this chapter.

Here are some of the lessons from the first nine chapters:

- The nation's schools of education tend to operate out of the intellectual tradition that regards children as natural learners best left to discover what they need to know on their own, and to think critically about what they discern. This so-called learner-centered approach contrasts with teacher-centered instruction, which may entail a certain degree of memorization and drill until the basics are mastered. The diligent sifting of research done by Jeanne Chall during her lifetime showed clearly that for most pupils in most circumstances, teacher-centered or -directed instruction produced the greatest measurable gains in learning. Of course, those of the romantic tradition in the education schools do not regard test scores as a legitimate measure of educational value. But as surveys by the nonpartisan group Public Agenda have shown, the vast majority of parents disagree. They look for test score improvements.
- Once they have hit their stride teaching in their own classrooms, teachers tend to adjust the theories they were taught in college to the practical realities they discover on their own. Some teachers continue to subscribe to the learner-centered tradition, while others discard it as impractical and go to their own version of direct teaching. Some teachers blend the approaches. But whether they subscribe to the learner-centered or teacher-centered approach, most teachers told us they thought their schools of education should have stressed more practical lessons applicable to real-life classrooms, and should have dwelled on theory far less. Almost

without exception, the many teachers surveyed said that the clinical portion of their training—practice teaching, which is a form of mentor-assisted preparation—was the most helpful part of their preparation.

- Power over teacher training and certification is wielded by a public monopoly that zealously guards its prerogatives and refuses to abide constructive criticism. Defenders of this inbred, elitist system seek to smother all reform in musty reports purporting to show that teachers who are products of this certification mill are more effective than teachers who manage to get past the gatekeepers without the prescribed heavy load of education courses. However, the record is far more mixed than they will admit. There are plenty of indications that teachers who are liberal arts graduates with no pedagogical schooling can do, and have done, just fine, thank you, as high school teachers.

- The proposition just stated should not surprise, given that professors in the great universities are hired without having to present bean counters a list of how-to-teach courses they have completed. Why should a scholar in English literature be perfectly fit to teach in academe and even to win tenure and an endowed professorship, yet be regarded as unqualified to stand before a high school English class unless he or she can show the requisite pedagogical courses completed? Of course, such a scholar also would be welcomed at the best of privately run high schools, where principals are free to hire the brightest candidates they can find, without regard to certifiers' course-counting.

- Journalists are in many respects teachers. The best of them do high-quality work that helps educate the public. Yet, staffs of newspapers and magazines come together differently than do public-school faculties. An editorial department may consist of a journalism major in one office, a history major in another, a former Peace Corps volunteer here, a former business entrepreneur there. Journalism schools serve a purpose in training a core of entry-level reporters for print and electronic media, and in providing continuing education opportunities for those in the media business. However, the Journalism schools or schools of communications do not function as the gatekeepers to a closed profession. Diversity of background and viewpoint tend to be prized in journalism, but that's not the case in bureaucratically controlled K–12 education. Yet children could benefit from having teachers who brought to their teaching a wide variety of work experiences and worldviews.

- There are two sharply opposed camps in the contention over how best to reform teacher preparation and licensing. One side calls for deregulation and decentralization so that public-school principals can act much as private-school principals do in recruiting and hiring their own faculties. The other side seeks to centralize power over the gates to teaching all the more, by making all teacher training subject to certification by one organization,

NCATE (National Council for Accreditation of Teacher Education), and by accelerating the growth of one national certification board for teachers, the NBPTS (National Board for Professional Teaching Standards), which clearly favors learner-centered over teacher-centered methods.

- The NBPTS is the showpiece of the centralizers' prescribed bill of fare. Yet, in its first 15 years, the NBPTS yielded little, if any, solid evidence that teachers who win its blessing, largely by submitting videotapes of themselves in action in the classroom, are any more effective in raising their students' achievement than are non-board-certified teachers. If certification has not been useful in producing better teachers, is there any reason to believe that supercertification would have any better result?

- The world is moving away from the use of centralized authority to control intellectual activity. The movement is toward free markets and innovation. The education market is changing rapidly as private providers move in to offer everything from tutoring to, yes, teacher training. Distance learning in higher education has been followed by cyber charter schools in the K–12 realm, although the same education establishment that clings to teacher certification bitterly resists such liberating strides. As a former speechwriter for Vice President Albert Gore, Daniel H. Pink argues persuasively in *Free Agent Nation,* "more free agent teachers and more free agent students will create tremendous liquidity in the learning market— with the Internet serving as matchmaker and market maker for this new marketplace of learning" (Pink, 2001: 257).

- Teachers are beginning to discover that school choice can benefit them as well as parents and children. In a competitive education industry, the services of a capable teacher can acquire increased market value. An enterprising teacher might sell his or her services to a home-school co-op, or teachers might band together to organize their own public charter school where they can put their own convictions about superior teaching to work. The feds are backing establishment by local folks of these innovative public schools with millions of dollars of new appropriations. In Philadelphia, the state and local governments are turning to private management to help rescue several dozen chronically failing public schools. New ways of delivering education are coming to the fore everywhere, making the old barriers to teaching all the more obsolete. The era of the entrepreneurial teacher may be about to dawn.

A new way of thinking about building better teachers (and clearing them for employment) can come from thinking about two very different states—New Jersey and Tennessee—in combination. These archetypes of Northern industrialism and Southern agrarianism may each have a major piece of a thoroughgoing reform of teacher licensing and hiring.

First, think New Jersey when pondering how to open up the gates to teaching without destroying the best of what the current system has to offer. New Jersey's system is dual track, but both tracks end with new teachers having enough of a common grounding to avoid hard feelings or inequities. Those who have gone to the schools of education because they want to become teachers can still become teachers on the traditional track, but they do so with far fewer education courses than in the past and with a major in the liberal arts or sciences. And as part of their collegiate preparation to be a teacher, they are put under the tutelage of an experienced teacher. Meanwhile, on the alternate track, liberal arts graduates who haven't been to education school at all can also be hired as teachers and they, too, are immediately put under the supervision of a mentor. Hence, on-the-job training is a common experience for all new teachers, no matter what their backgrounds.

Now, think Tennessee and in particular its Value-Added Assessment System for a logical next step to bolster teaching. When men and women of promising talent come into the classroom from a variety of routes and receive helpful advice from an experienced teacher/mentor, their journey has just begun. Why not use the most sophisticated data analysis to follow year by year how much they are helping each child progress—how much "value" they are adding? Education is about steady improvement, whether the learner starts from a very low or an advanced level of knowledge and understanding.

Critics suggest there are too many uncertainties about value-added assessment to use it as a yardstick of teacher effectiveness. They point out that there can be errors in testing scores, and that students' gains sometimes are attributable to factors outside the control of teachers or schools. Additionally, University of Massachusetts economist Dale Ballou—an astute critic of teacher union–influenced evaluation mechanisms like the NBPTS—expressed qualms because value-added data in Tennessee showed that teachers of some subjects, notably reading, fell within an average range of effectiveness, with (for reading) only 5 percent either noticeably better or worse than average. He argues that such consistency makes it scarcely worth the effort to identify teachers for rewarding (Ballou, 2002). However, his analysis ignores the possibility that so many teachers may be "average" precisely because of the widespread dominance of such progressive teaching methods as Whole Language. A value-added approach could be valuable precisely in determining what distinguishes those small numbers of teachers of reading (or other subjects) who excel.

As noted in chapter 8, the Tennessee version of Value-Added Assessment addresses such concerns as scores being affected by factors (e.g., socioeconomic status) over which the schools have no control. No system of statistical analysis can ever be completely free of what those in the trade call "noise," or the rest of us might call "bugs." But Anita A. Summers, a professor emeritus of public policy and management at the Wharton School, makes the great point that value-added assessment should be measured against the alternatives, which "are simply untenable" (Summers, 2002). One alternative is to judge the impact of teaching subjectively (i.e., by surveys of how much the students, parents, or other teachers liked a particular teacher). But that does not take into account whether learning advanced in measurable ways. As indicated by recollections of "best teachers" in chapter 2, teachers we most admire in retrospect may be those who years ago were most demanding, and not necessarily our favorites. Another alternative to a value-added focus on improvement is to construct an arbitrary standard to define adequate performance. But, as Summers wisely notes, determining that threshold becomes a political issue. Those seeking rewards push for lower standards than do those responsible for the budgets. In the ensuing tug-of-war, focus is lost on how much teachers have helped their students progress from where they started.

To some advocates, building a better teacher doesn't have to entail complex value-added formulas or new forms of preparation and certification. All that is necessary, they argue, is a major increase in the level of teacher pay. If you pay them handsomely, they will come. However, if teachers continue to be paid in an unprofessional way, according to seniority-based step salary schedules negotiated by their unions that take no account of individual merit, it is doubtful that bright people considering careers will look at teaching as a desirable professional pursuit. The current system rewards brilliance, mediocrity, and outright incompetence equally.

What is needed, as Bryan C. Hassel has argued in a study for the Progressive Policy Institute, is a two-way bargain: improve teachers' pay and simultaneously reform the system by which they are paid. "We should reward teachers not just for experience, but for the skills, knowledge, and, ultimately, the performance they bring into their classrooms." Teachers might receive pay boosts for being willing to accept assignment to high-poverty, low-achieving schools, or for having math and science expertise that is in woefully short supply in K–12 education (Hassel, 2002: 2–3). But surely the best way, the most productive way, to reward great teaching is to reward teaching that produces verifiable results, and particularly year-to-year achievement gains for students. In this way, the value-added concept could be a boon to effective teachers and genuine professionalization.

Others make the argument that if you want better teachers, test them before placing them in front of a class. Test them for their teacher know-how, their command of the language, their knowledge of their subject; test them every which way to Sunday. Proof of rigorous subject-matter preparation is a key element of the federal Education Department's new guidelines for ensuring teacher quality. That proof can come from passing a "rigorous state test" or from presenting outstanding academic credentials. This approach sounds incontrovertible and is certainly a major improvement over testing teachers for their ability to spout pedagogical mush, but serious problems will arise if the federal government becomes heavily involved in how teachers are assessed. Education is constitutionally and properly a state and local responsibility in the United States. It would be dangerous as well as inefficient to concentrate power over teaching in the hands of an education ministry or education czar.

Political Washington is attempting to respect those bounds by using its fiscal and regulatory clout merely to nudge local policy in the direction of reform. Capitol Hill and the White House have both homed in on teacher quality as an area in need of particularly strong nudging. Hence, the feds call on the states to come up with their own tests of teachers (as well as of students in grades 3–8 under NCLB) rather than prescribing national tests. (And thank God for that!) However, one lesson learned under the truth-in-teacher-training provisions of the Higher Education Act as reauthorized in 1998 is that definitions of "rigorous" evaluation vary wildly from one place to another, depending on how desperately officials want to keep future teachers in the pipeline as well as protect their own professional reputations. The bottom line is that government tests of academic knowledge could be rather watered down in some states, depending on the political environment.

In the end, why not trust the market to bring education consumers superior schools and stellar teachers? So much could improve if only parents could choose their children's schools.

If K–12 education were market-based, it is probable that most parents would want basic assurances regarding the teachers being recruited to their school. A bachelor's degree, with a major in a genuine academic discipline related to what the teacher would be teaching, would be a basic requirement. So might a criminal background check. Parents might want their principal to have the leeway to administer a test of knowledge or literacy to teacher candidates, or if the principal had a track record as a successful manager, they might just trust his or her judgment, particularly if the principal would be assigning mentors to supervise the new teachers. It is doubtful that a score on a test imposed by a remote bureaucracy would mean all that much to the parent-consumers. Common sense instructs us that some people who score high on tests can't teach their way out of a paper bag, while others who may not shine on various psychometric devices can get children fired up about learning. Consumer choice could work wonders in bringing common sense to the little red schoolhouses of the country.

Ultimately, the testing that would really count would be that showing how much students had improved year to year to year—how much value had been added to their learning. With market-based education, teachers who can consistently add that value to their students' learning will themselves acquire added value. Their services will be in demand, and as competitors come calling for them, they will begin to reap the rewards they so greatly deserve.

# References

Allen, Anne Wallace. 2001. Associated Press interview. *Rutland* (Vermont) *Herald* (November 23).

Andrews, Lewis M. 2002. *Choices for Disabled Kids: Lessons from Abroad.* Hartford, Conn.: Yankee Institute.

Angus, David L., and Jeffrey Mirel, eds. 2001. *Professionalism and the Public Good: A Brief History of Teacher Certification.* Washington, D.C.: Thomas B. Fordham Foundation.

Archer, Jeff. 2002. "National Board Is Pressed to Prove Certified Teachers Make Difference." *Education Week* (January 30).

Ballou, Dale. 2002. "Sizing up Test Scores." *Education Next* (Summer).

Ballou, Dale, and Michael Podgursky. 1997. "Reforming Teacher Training and Recruitment." *Government Union Review* 17, no. 4.

Ballou, Dale, and Michael Podgursky. 1999. "Teacher Training and Licensure: A Layman's Guide." In *Better Teachers, Better Schools*, edited by Marci Kanstoroom and Chester E. Finn, Jr. Washington, D.C.: Thomas B. Fordham Foundation.

Barzun, Jacques. 1992. *Begin Here: The Forgotten Condition of Teaching and Learning.* Chicago and London: University of Chicago Press.

Basinger, Julianne. 2000. "Colleges Widen Alternate Routes to Teacher Certification: 'Career Switchers' Flock to Programs That Offer Practical Experience in Classrooms." *Chronicle of Higher Education* (January 14).

Berliner, David C., and Bruce J. Biddle. 1995. *The Manufactured Crisis: Myths, Fraud, and the Attack on America's Public Schools.* Reading, Mass.: Addison-Wesley.

Bestor, Arthur. 1953. *Educational Wastelands: The Retreat from Learning in our Public Schools.* Urbana and Chicago: University of Illinois Press.

Blair, Julie. 2001. "New Accreditor Gaining Toehold in Teacher Ed." *Education Week* (May 23).

Blair, Julie. 2002. "Teacher-Trainers Fear a Backfire from New ESEA." *Education Week* (March 6).

Bond, Lloyd, et al. 2000. *The Certification System of the National Board for Professional Teaching Standards: A Construct and Consequential Validity Study.* Greensboro: Center for Educational Research and Evaluation, University of North Carolina at Greensboro. http:// www.edpolicy.org/research/NPEAT/nbpts2.pdf.

Bradley, Ann. 2000. "For-Profits Tapping into Teacher Training." *Education Week* (March 29).

Brouillette, Matthew J. 2001. *A Privatized School Monopoly Is No Better Than a Government School Monopoly.* Midland, Mich.: Mackinac Center for Public Policy.

Caliber.com. 2001. "Caliber Learning Network Joins with Teachers College, Columbia University, and Sylvan in Live eLearning Institute." Press release, June 14. www.caliber.com.

Candidate's Guide. 2001. *A Candidate's Guide to National Board Certification 2001–02.* Washington, D.C.: American Federation of Teachers and National Education Association.

Carnine, Douglas. 2000. *Why Education Experts Resist Effective Practices (and What It Would Take to Make Education More Like Medicine).* Washington, D.C.: Thomas B. Fordham Foundation.

Carter, Samuel Casey. 2000. *No Excuses: Lessons from 21 High-Performing, High-Poverty Schools.* Washington, D.C.: Heritage Foundation.

Chall, Jeanne S. 2000. *The Academic Achievement Challenge: What Really Works in the Classroom?* New York: Guilford Press.

Chandler, Louis. 1999. *Traditional Schools, Progressive Schools: Do Parents Have a Choice? A Case Study of Ohio.* Washington, D.C.: Thomas B. Fordham Foundation.

Clowes, George A. 2001. "Who Tells Teachers They Can Teach?" *School Reform News* (September): 20.

Clowes, George A. 2002. "Productivity in Public Education." *School Reform News* (March). http://heartland.org/educationMar02/inputs/htm.

Coeyman, Marjorie. 2001. "America's Widening Teacher Gap." *Christian Science Monitor* (July 17).

Committee for Economic Development (CED). 2000. *Measuring What Matters: Using Assessment and Accountability to Improve Student Learning.* New York: Research and Policy Committee, CED.

Cremin, Lawrence A. 1961. *The Transformation of the School: Progressivism in American Education 1876–1957.* New York: Vintage Books.

Darling-Hammond, Linda. 1997. *The Right to Learn: A Blueprint for Creating Schools That Work.* San Francisco: Jossey-Bass.

Darling-Hammond, Linda. 2001. *The Research and the Rhetoric on Teacher*

*Certification: A Response to "Teacher Certification Reconsidered."* New York: National Commission on Teaching and America's Future.

Darling-Hammond, Linda, Arthur E. Wise, and Stephen P. Klein. 1999. *A License to Teach: Raising Standards for Teaching.* San Francisco: Jossey-Bass.

Dean, Mensah M., and Chris Brennan. 2002. "For 70 Schools, Let the Reforms Begin." *Philadelphia Daily News* (April 18).

Dewey, John. 1944 [1916]. *Democracy and Education: An Introduction to the Philosophy of Education.* New York: Free Press.

Donsky, Paul. 2001. "Teach for Georgia Officials Say Program's Turnout 'Extraordinary.'" *Atlanta Journal-Constitution* (July 4).

Education Consumers Clearinghouse (ECC) Consultants Network. 2001. *Teacher Certification Isn't Working.* www.education-consumers.com.

Evers, Bill. 2001. *What Do Tests Tell Us?* Hoover Institution Weekly Essay, August 20–27. www.hoover.Stanford.edu/pubaffairs/we/current/evers_080/.pdf.

Feistritzer, C. Emily. 1999. *The Making of a Teacher: A Report on Teacher Preparation in the U.S.* Washington, D.C.: Center for Education Information.

Feistritzer, C. Emily, and David T. Chester. 2002. *Alternative Teacher Certification: A State-by-State Analysis 2002.* Washington, D.C.: National Center for Education Information.

Forstmann, Theodore J. 1999. "A Competitive Vision for American Education." *Imprimis* (Hillsdale College) 28, no. 9 (September).

Franciosi, Robert. 2001. *No Voice, No Exit: The Inefficiency of America's Public Schools.* Dallas: Institute for Policy Innovation.

Gehring, John. 2001. "U.S. Seen Losing Edge on Education Measures." *Education Week* (April 4): 3.

Goldhaber, Dan D., and Dominic J. Brewer. 1999. "Teacher Licensing and Student Achievement." In *Better Teachers, Better Schools,* edited by Marci Kanstoroom and Chester E. Finn, Jr. Washington, D.C.: Thomas B. Fordham Foundation.

Goldhaber, Dan D., and Dominic J. Brewer. 2000. *Educational Evaluation and Policy Analysis* (Summer), as cited in "In Short," *Education Week* (October 18).

Greene, Jay P. 2001. *High School Graduation Rates in the United States.* Washington, D.C.: Black Alliance for Educational Options.

Hassel, Bryan C. 2002. *Better Pay for Better Teaching: Making Teacher Compensation Pay Off in the Age of Accountability.* Washington, D.C.: Progressive Policy Institute.

Haycock, Kati. 1998. *Good Teaching Matters . . . a Lot.* Washington, D.C.: Education Trust. http://www.edtrust.org.

Hess, Frederick M. 2001. *Tear Down This Wall: The Case for a Radical*

*Overhaul of Teacher Certification.* Washington, D.C.: Progressive Policy Institute.

Hill, David. 2000. "He's Got Your Number." *Teacher* (May). www.teachermagazine.org/tm/tm_printstory.cfm?slug=08sanders.h11.

Hirsch, E. D., Jr. 1996. *The Schools We Need and Why We Don't Have Them.* New York: Doubleday.

Holland, Robert. 2000. *Use the Free Market to Land the Best Teachers for America's Children.* Arlington, Va.: Lexington Institute.

Holland, Robert. 2001. "U.S. Students Trounced in Int'l Science Match." *School Reform News* (February). www.heartland.org/education/febol/ timss.htm. Retrieved December 3, 2001. Copy of full report, *Pursuing Excellence: Comparisons of International Eighth-Grade Mathematics and Science Achievement from a U.S. Perspective, 1995 and 1999,* at http:// nces.ed.gov/timss.

Holland, Robert. 2002a. "Catastrophic Public School Failure Threatens National Security." *Middle American News* (January): 6.

Holland, Robert. 2002b. *The Rise of Home Schooling Among African-Americans.* Arlington, Va.: Lexington Institute.

Holland, Robert, and Don Soifer. 2000. *Waste in Education: Public Schools Produce Low Literacy Return for the Dollars Spent.* Indianapolis, Ind.: Milton and Rose D. Friedman Foundation.

Horn, Joseph M. 1999. *A Critical Look at Texas Colleges of Education.* San Antonio: Texas Public Policy Foundation.

Hoxby, Caroline M. 2001. "Changing the Profession." *Education Next* (Spring).

Ingersoll, Richard M. 2001. *Teacher Turnover, Teacher Shortages, and the Organization of Schools.* Teaching Quality Policy Brief no. 3. Seattle: Center for the Study of Teaching and Policy, University of Washington.

Izumi, Lance T., with K. Gwynne Coburn. 2001. *Facing the Classroom Challenge: Teacher Quality and Teacher Training in California's Schools of Education.* San Francisco: Pacific Research Institute for Public Policy.

Kanstoroom, Marci. 2000. *Value-Added Assessment: Ready for Prime Time?* Washington, D.C.: Education Leaders Council.

Kanstoroom, Marci, and Chester E. Finn, Jr., eds. 1999. *Better Teachers, Better Schools.* Washington, D.C.: Thomas B. Fordham Foundation.

Klagholz, Leo. 2000. *Growing Better Teachers in the Garden State: New Jersey's "Alternate Route" to Teacher Certification.* Washington, D.C.: Thomas B. Fordham Foundation.

Koerner, James D. 1963. *The Miseducation of American Teachers.* Baltimore: Penguin Books.

Koetzsch, Ronald E. 1997. *The Parents' Guide to Alternatives in Education.* Boston and London: Shambhala.

Kohn, Alfie. 1999. *The Schools Our Children Deserve: Moving Beyond Tradi-*

*tional Classrooms and "Tougher Standards."* Boston and New York: Houghton Mifflin.

Kopp, Wendy. 2001. *One Day, All Children: The Unlikely Triumph of Teach for America and What I Learned Along the Way.* New York: Public Affairs.

Kramer, Rita. 2000. *Ed School Follies: The Miseducation of American Teachers.* Lincoln, Neb.: iUniverse.com. Originally published New York: Free Press, 1991.

Leef, George C., ed. 2002. *Educating Teachers: The Best Minds Speak Out.* Washington, D.C.: American Council of Trustees and Alumni.

Lieberman, Myron. 1997. *The Teacher Unions: How the NEA and AFT Sabotage Reform and Hold Students, Parents, Teachers, and Taxpayers Hostage to Bureaucracy.* New York: Free Press.

Lips, Carrie. 2000. *"Edupreneurs": A Survey of For-Profit Education.* Policy Analysis no. 236. Washington, D.C.: Cato Institute.

Long, Diane, and Michael Cass. 2001. "Analyst Rocks Education Boat." *Nashville Tennessean* (January 11). www.tennessean.com/local/archieves/01/01/01776708.shtml.

Loveless, Tom. "The Use and Misuse of Research in Educational Reform." In *Brookings Papers on Education Policy*, edited by Diane Ravitch. Washington, D.C.: Brookings Institution.

Mac Donald, Heather. 1999. *Why Johnny's Teachers Can't Teach.* New York: The City Journal.

Manzo, Kathleen Kennedy. 2002. "U.S. History Again Stumps Senior Class." *Education Week* (May 15). Full report at http://nces.ed.gov/nationsreportcard/ushistory/results.

Mathews, Jay. 2003. "Education Effort Meets Resistance: Leaders Say Teacher Certification Test Was Sabotaged." *The Washington Post* (June 10). http://washingtonpost.com/wp-dyn/articles/A367972003June10.html

Mencken, H. L. 1928. "The War on Intelligence." In *A Second Mencken Chrestomathy.* New York: Vintage, 1994 (reprint).

Moats, Louisa Cook. 1995. "The Missing Foundation in Teacher Preparation." *The American Educator* (Summer).

Moats, Louisa Cook. 2000. *Whole Language Lives On: The Illusion of "Balanced" Reading Instruction.* Washington, D.C.: Thomas B. Fordham Foundation.

National Commission on Excellence in Education. 1983. *A Nation at Risk: The Imperative for Educational Reform. A Report to the Nation and the Secretary of Education.* Washington, D.C. http://www.ed.gov/pubs/NatAtRisk/risk.html.

NCES. 2001a. *The Nation's Report Card: Fourth-Grade Reading 2000.* Washington, D.C.: National Assessment of Educational Progress. http://nces.ed.gov/nationsreportcard/reading.

NCES. 2001b. *The Nation's Report Card: Mathematics 2000.* Washington, D.C.: National Assessment of Educational Progress. http://nces.ed.gov/nationsreportcard/mathematics.

NCES. 2001c. *The Nation's Report Card: Science Highlights 2000.* Washington, D.C.: National Assessment of Educational Progress. http://nces.ed.gov/pubsearch/pubsinfo.asp?pubid=2002452. Retrieved November 23, 2001.

NCES. 2001d. *Pursuing Excellence: Comparisons of International Eighth-Grade Mathematics and Science Achievement from a U.S. Perspective, 1995 and 1999.* Third International Mathematics and Science Study—Repeat (TIMSS-R). http://nces.ed.gov.timss.

NCTAF. 1996. *What Matters Most: Teaching for America's Future.* New York: National Commission on Teaching and America's Future.

NCTAF. 2001. "National Commission on Teaching and America's Future Refutes Abell Foundation Report." Press release. http://www.nctaf.org/whatsnew/abell_release.htm. Retrieved October 11, 2001.

NRP. 2000. *Teaching Children to Read: An Evidence-Based Assessment of the Scientific Research Literature on Reading and Its Implications for Reading Instruction.* Washington, D.C.: National Reading Panel.

Office.com. 2001. "Why Sylvan Chose to Invest in Walden" (March 9). www.office.com.

O'Keeffe, Dennis J. 1990. *The Wayward Elite: A Critique of British Teacher-Education.* London: Adam Smith Institute.

Palmer, Joy A., ed. 2001. *Fifty Modern Thinkers in Education: From Piaget to the Present.* London and New York: Routledge.

Pink, Daniel H. 2001. *Free Agent Nation: The Future of Working for Yourself.* New York: Warner Books.

Podgursky, Michael. 2001. "Should States Subsidize National Certification?" *Education Week* (April 11): 38, 40–41.

Podgursky, Michael, and Dale Ballou. 2001. *Personnel Policy in Charter Schools.* Washington, D.C.: Thomas B. Fordham Foundation.

Policy Brief. 2001. *The Best Teachers: Getting Them, Keeping Them.* Alexandria, Va.: Foundation Endowment.

Ponessa, Jeanne. 1997. "Despite Rocky Road, Ed-School Accreditation Effort on a Roll." *Education Week* (June 18). http://www.edweek.org/ew/newstory.cfm?slug=38ncate.h16. Retrieved June 18, 2002.

Public Agenda. 1994. *First Things First: What Americans Expect from the Public Schools.* New York: Public Agenda.

Public Agenda. 1997. *Different Drummers: How Teachers of Teachers View Public Education.* New York: Public Agenda.

Ravitch, Diane. 2000. *Left Back: A Century of Failed School Reforms.* New York: Simon & Schuster.

Raymond, Margaret, with Stephen H. Fletcher and Javier Luque. 2001. *Teach for America: An Evaluation of Teacher Differences and Student*

*Outcomes in Houston, Texas.* CREDO. Stanford: Hoover Institution. Thomas B. Fordham Foundation, Project Sponsor.

Rousseau, Jean-Jacques. 1993. *Emile,* translated by Barbara Foxley. London: Everyman.

Rudman, Warren, and Gary Hart. 1999. *New World Coming: American Security in the 21st Century.* U.S. Commission on National Security/ 21st Century, Phase I Report. Washington, D.C.

Rudman, Warren, and Gary Hart. 2001. *Road Map for National Security: Imperative for Change.* U.S. Commission on National Security/21st Century, Phase III Report. Washington, D.C.

Sanders, William L. 2000. "Value-Added Assessment from Student Achievement Data: Opportunities and Hurdles." *Journal of Personnel Evaluation in Education* (July 21).

Sanders, William L., and Sandra P. Horn. 1994. "The Tennessee Value-Added Assessment System (TVAAS): Mixed Method Methodology in Educational Assessment." *Journal of Personnel Evaluation in Education.*

Scarborough, Melanie. 2001. *Charter Schools Succeed Despite Dirty Tricks.* Arlington, Va.: Lexington Institute.

Schemo, Diana Jean. 2001. "U.S. Students Prove Middling on a 32-Nation Test." *New York Times* (December 5): A21.

Secretary's Annual Report. 2002. *Meeting the Highly Qualified Teachers Challenge: The Secretary's Annual Report on Teacher Quality.* Washington, D.C.: Office of Postsecondary Education, Office of Policy Planning and U.S. Department of Education.

Slater, Cliff. 2002. "DOE: Rigor Mortis Has Set In." *Honolulu Advertiser* (January 24).

Steidler, Paul. 1999. "Freedom to Thrive: The Opportunities for Teachers from Parental Choice." Unpublished paper prepared for the Milton and Rose D. Friedman Foundation.

Stephenson, Frederick J., Jr., ed. 2001. *Extraordinary Teachers: The Essence of Excellent Teaching.* Kansas City, Miss.: Andrews McMeel.

Stone, J. E. 1998a. "'Different Drummers' and Teacher Training: A Disharmony That Impairs Schooling." *Education Week* (February 4).

Stone, J. E. 1998b. *What Is Value-Added Assessment and Why Do We Need It?* Alexandria, Va.: Foundation Endowment.

Stone, J. E. 1999. "The National Council for Accreditation of Teacher Education: Whose Standards?" In *Better Teachers, Better Schools,* edited by Marci Kanstoroom and Chester E. Finn, Jr. Washington, D.C.: Thomas B. Fordham Foundation.

Stone, J. E. 2002. *Value-Added Achievement Gains of NBPTS-Certified Teachers in Tennessee: A Brief Report.* Education Consumers Consultants Network. http://www.education-consumers.com/briefs/ StoneNBPTS.shtm.

Stronge, James H., and Pamela D. Tucker. 2001. *Teacher Evaluation and Student Achievement.* Education Consumers Consultants Network. www.educationconsumers.com/briefs/march2001.shtm.

Summers, Anita A. 2002. "Expert Measures." *Education Next* (Summer).

Symonds, William C. 2001. "Edison: Pass, not Fail." *Business Week* (July 9).

Thuermer, Kitty. 1999. "In Defense of the Progressive School: An Interview with Alfie Kohn." *Independent School.* www.alfiekohn.org/teaching/idotps.htm/.

TIMSS-R. 2001. Pursuing Excellence: Comparisons of International Eighth-Grade Mathematics and Science Achievement from a U.S. Perspective, 1995 and 1999. National Center for Education Statistics. http://nces.ed.gov.timss.

Von Kohorn, Ken. 2002. "The Economy Soars, Schools Drag." *American Enterprise* (April/May).

Walsh, Kate. 2001. *Teacher Certification Reconsidered: Stumbling for Quality.* Baltimore: Abell Foundation. http://www.abell.org/pubsitems/ed_cert_1101.pdf.

Walsh, Mark. 2000. "Edison to Explore Expansion into Teacher Preparation." *Education Week* (May 3).

Walsh, Mark. 2002. "Tutoring Services See Opportunity in New Law." *Education Week* (January 23).

Wilcox, Danielle Dunne. 1999. "The National Board for Professional Teaching Standards: Can It Live up to Its Promise?" In *Better Teachers, Better Schools,* edited by Marci Kanstoroom and Chester E. Finn, Jr. Washington, D.C.: Thomas B. Fordham Foundation.

Wong, Harry K. 2001. "Mentoring Can't Do It All: New Teachers Learn Best from Systematic Induction Programs." *Education Week* (August 8): 46, 50.

Yecke, Cheri Pierson. 2002. Presentation to forum "Next Steps for Education Reform in the Old Dominion" (May 14). Copies of the videotaped presentation are available from the Lexington Institute in Arlington, Va.: (703) 522-5828.

*Zelman* v. *Simmons-Harris,* 536 U.S., 00-1751 (June 27, 2002).

# Index

## About the Author

ROBERT GRAY HOLLAND is a Senior Fellow with the Lexington Institute in the Washington, D.C., area. As a newspaper columnist and editor, Holland won the H. L. Mencken Award for his incisive writing on education. He is prominent among school reformers seeking the nationwide spread of greater choice in education. His articles have appeared in such journals as *Policy Review*, the *Howard University Law Journal*, and *USA Today*, as well as in major newspapers. His 1995 book, *Not With My Child, You Don't*, told the story of parental opposition to mandatory school restructuring.